Explore Ko Samui 31

Survival Guide 141

Special Features

Welcome to Ko Samui

The largest of a family of three spectacular islands luring millions of tourists every year with powder-soft sands and emerald waters, Ko Samui is the oldest sibling who made it big. Here high-class resorts operate with Swiss efficiency as uniformed butlers cater to every whim, but there's plenty of hammock-lazing and bungalow beach life too.

POCKET

KO SAMUI

TOP SIGHTS · LOCAL EXPERIENCES

Contents

Plan Your Trip

Ko Samui beach (p60)
DAPHNUSIA/SHUTTERSTOCK ©

Hat Lamai (p63), Ko Samui

Top Experiences

Wat Plai Laem

The best-looking temple on Ko Samui. **p35**

Fisherman's Village

Ko Samui's most fascinating village.
p36

Mae Nam Beach

Sedate beach life, vibrant settlement.
p83

Ko Pha-Ngan's Hidden Beaches

The island's quietest moments.
p106

Full Moon Party

All-night, alcohol-fuelled rave. **p108**

JOEL CARILLET/GETTY IMAGES ©

FAR LEFT: VLAD61/SHUTTERSTOCK ©, LEFT: INGRAM PUBLISHING/GETTY IMAGES ©

Diving off Ko Tao

Top dive sites in Thailand. **p128**

Ao Tanot

Beautiful bay, fab snorkelling, seclusion. **p130**

West Coast Sunsets

Ko Tao at its best. **p126**

Na Muang Waterfalls

Ko Samui's most famous falls. **p64**

FAR RIGHT: JHOLGER METTE/GETTY IMAGES ©. RIGHT: DMITRIYVPETRENKO/GETTY IMAGES ©. BELOW: LONELY PLANET/GETTY IMAGES ©

Ang Thong Marine National Park

Primordial, idyllic island landscape. **p102**

Eating

Many visitors are lured to Ko Samui by the promise of a gastronomic adventure and the island's restaurants step up to the plate. Indeed, it may matter little if you hunt out the snazziest resort restaurant or the cheapest shack on the beach: dishes are waiting that will simply blow your taste buds away.

Ko Samui Flavours

The island makes the most of its ample supply of fresh seafood as well as the various culinary influences of southern Thai cuisine. Cloves, cinnamon and cardamom are some of the spices from Indonesia and India that are fed into the aromatic makeup of local dishes such as *gang mát·sà·mân* (Muslim curry) and *kôw mòk gài* (chicken biryani).

The Kôw Gaang Gang

Influenced by the mainland, Samui is peppered with *kôw gaang* (rice and curry) shops, usually just wooden shacks displaying large metal pots of southern Thai-style curries. They are one of the handiest pit stops for lunch or a snack while on the road. *Kôw gaang* shops are easily found along the Ring Rd (Rte 4169) and sell out of the good stuff by 1pm.

Nut for Coconuts

It's no surprise that Samui's most famous natural produce finds its way into a medley of dishes. There's sweet coconut jam to spread on your croissants in the morning. *Wai kôo·a* is a spicy and sour coconut-based curry featuring octopus. *Tom kha* is a flavoursome chicken soup made with coconut milk, lemongrass, lime juice, ginger, fish sauce and chilli paste.

AS FOOD STUDIO/SHUTTERSTOCK ©

Best Restaurants

Barracuda Exquisite Mediterranean dishes in a romantic setting. (p41)

Hemingway's on the Beach First-rate Thai dishes, beachfront. (p74)

Fisherman's Restaurant Gorgeous Thai menu and Ko Pha-Ngan beach-side perspective. (p120)

Pepenero Stand-out Italian menu, welcoming staff. (p86)

Dining on the Rocks Invigorating menu and a peerless setting. (p42)

Best for Views

Dining on the Rocks The ultimate star-gazing experience. (p42)

Five Islands One of Ko Samui's most memorable dinners. (p98)

Fisherman's Restaurant Very romantic dinners. (p120)

Hemingway's on the Beach Sunsets and sea (p74)

Best International Fare

Farmer Choice inland setting with views of the hills and fine food to match. (p87)

Barracuda Supreme Mediterranean menu in a seductive night-time environment. (p41)

Radiance Wholesome, healthy food with lovely sea views. (p74)

Barracuda Restaurant & Bar Ko Tao's finest fusion dishes. (p137)

Zazen Romantic bliss, on a plate. (p41)

Top Tips

o Open-air markets and food stalls are among the most popular places for Thais to eat.

o The phrase 'I'm vegetarian' in Thai is *pŏm gin jair* (for men) or *dì·chăn gin jair* (for women).

Drinking & Nightlife

Samui's biggest party spot is brash and noisy Hat Chaweng. Lamai and Bo Phut come in second and third respectively, while the rest of the island is generally quiet, with drinking usually focused on resort bars. For sunset cocktails, hit the west coast, or parts of the north coast.

Party Island?

Ko Samui aspires to a thumping Ibiza party scene, but most nights it's pretty tame and boozy, with a touch of port town seediness thrown in. Most party-goers wait for the full moon before making the journey to Ko Pha-Ngan for the monthly beach shindigs, with boat operators shuttling party-goers to Hat Rin and back.

Bar Zones & Beer

On Ko Samui, Chaweng is the undisputed hub of the action. Lamai and Bo Phut have a few bars and clubs but are more in the slow lane, while things are pretty quiet in Mae Nam. Depressing hostess bars cluster in Chaweng.

Thai beers include Singha (pronounced 'sing') and Chang. Imported beers are widely available and the enterprising Bees Knees Brewpub (p58) brews its own fabulous beer. Wines, mainly from Europe and Australia, are widely available at upmarket restaurants.

Annoyances, Dangers & Restrictions

When the army is on Ko Samui, bars island-wide may be forced to close at 1am, instead of later. During certain Buddhist festivals, you may find alcohol difficult to obtain for a few days. Watch out for fake alcohol on Ko Pha-Ngan, especially during the full moon. Despite the temptation, never drink and drive: on a motorbike or scooter, it's a lethal combination.

KATJA KREDER/GETTY IMAGES ©

Best Bars

Coco Tam's The ultimate beach bar. (p43)

Air Bar Make it a date at sunset. (p99)

Fizz Ko Tao's winning sunset bar. (p127)

Woobar Supreme chill-out zone. (p44)

Belgian Beer Bar Best beer on Ko Pha-Ngan. (p122)

Best Beach Bars

Coco Tam's The perfect finish to the day. (p43)

Fizz Hop into a beanbag and let the sunset and cocktails work their magic. (p127)

Ark Bar Party crowd, great sounds. (p59)

Secret Beach Bar Head here as the sun goes down. (p121)

Best for Views

Air Bar The best choice for a cocktail when the sun goes down. (p99)

Woobar Very good-looking and ultra-hip. (p44)

Jungle Club Getting up here is half the fun, but take it easy. (p56)

Coco Tam's Order up a cocktail and stare out on the waves. (p43)

Beryl Bar Simple, rough and ready, but delicious sunsets. (p88)

Secret Beach Bar Gorgeous and romantic, especially at sunset. (p121)

Best for Beer

Belgian Beer Bar Terrific selection on the west coast of Ko Pha-Ngan. (p122)

Tropical Murphy's Irish A much-loved mainstay of the Chaweng beer scene. (p59)

Bees Knees Brewpub Fantastic own-brewed beer. (p58)

Legends Pretty much the cheapest beer in Chaweng. (p58)

Best for Cocktails

Air Bar Fabulous setting matched by a winning cocktail menu. (p99)

Woobar Superb cocktail list and ravishing décor. (p44)

Fizz Superb drinks to go with killer views. (p127)

Coco Tam's Sink into a beanbag and lift your cocktail high. (p43)

Shopping

Ko Samui's upward mobility and mushrooming influx of visitors from mainland China have been a shopping bonanza for the island. Chaweng is still shopping central and you'll find all you need there if you want to sew up your buying duties in one go, but you'll find quality shopping enclaves and better prices if you shop around the island.

Togs & Threads

Clothing boutiques along Chaweng Beach Rd and in Fisherman's Village spill forth with not just rayon *faràng* sarongs, Chang beer T-shirts or tailor-made suits, but also an eye-catching range of cute and flirty dresses, perfect for a tropical setting and humid temperatures. Several boutiques in Chaweng also sell togs with designer labels, club-worthy outfits and silk shirts and tops. You'll find the top end at Central Festival and its environs. Fisherman's Village's boutiques are more artsy, easygoing and ethnic-chic, with natural cotton outfits and a slower pace.

Coconuts

Also keep an eye out for Samui's most famous export, the coconut, and the many health and beauty products made from it. Pharmacies and sundry shops across the island sell coconut oil, a natural skin moisturiser. Virgin coconut oil is also a hot superfood, often touted as a better cooking oil than olive or vegetable oils.

PARICHART80/SHUTTERSTOCK ©

Best Shopping

Fisherman's Village Walking Street Fun and colourful time to explore Fisherman's Village. (p46)

Baan Ngurn Very attractive and reasonably priced silver jewellery. (p46)

Hammock Cafe Plaeyuan Stop off for a coffee, buy a colourful hammock. (p138)

Central Festival Colourful mall at the heart of Chaweng. (p61)

Lamai Walking Street Night Market Full-on and vibrant night market. (p75)

Best Walking Streets & Night Markets

Fisherman's Village Walking Street The most vibrant Ko Samui walking street. (p46)

Mae Nam Walking Street On Thursday evenings on Ko Samui's north coast. (p83)

Thong Sala Walking Street Terrific Ko Pha-Ngan street market. (p123)

Lamai Walking Street Night Market Lamai at its busiest and most colourful. (p75)

Best for Handicrafts

Hammock Cafe Plaeyuan For all your Mlabri hand-woven colourful hammock needs. (p138)

Baan Ngurn Choice selection of silver jewellery in Fisherman's Village. (p46)

Nature Art Gallery Eye-catching range of jewellery in Chaweng. (p61)

The Wharf New open-air mall in Fisherman's Village. (p46)

Top Tip

◦ Don't go shopping in the company of touts, tour guides or friendly strangers as they will inevitably take a commission on anything you buy.

Beaches

*You don't have to stay in one place –
Ko Samui is small enough to beach-
hop with little difficulty. Chaweng is
the longest strip of sand and the main
draw, but after a while you'll want to
move on and start exploring. For the
best sand selection, head on to
the lower population densities of Ko
Pha-Ngan and Ko Tao.*

Chaweng & East Ko Samui

Chaweng is the most-visited beach: the northern part is rocky but subdued, the central area is crowded and busy, while in the south the small cove of Chaweng Noi offers a quiet respite. Further south, Lamai is a smaller and quieter version of Chaweng. Central Lamai is best for swimming, and southern Lamai is dotted with elephant-sized boulders.

North & West Ko Samui

The west coast boasts Taling Ngam and Lipa Noi, two pleasant swimming beaches for day-trippers from other parts of the island. Mae Nam is the best swimming beach on the north coast. The golden sand is soft and it is sheltered from high winds. The beach is steeply pitched, making the plunge a little abrupt for young swimmers. Bo Phut eases more gently into the sea but the sand is coarse and the water murky. In the northeast corner,

Ao Thong Sai is a real beauty with a deep cove, lush greenery and easygoing ambience. Swimming is good here but keep an eye out for submerged rocks.

Ko Tao & Ko Pha-Ngan

Ko Pha-Ngan and Ko Tao have far quieter and more remote beaches, but don't pitch up on the former during the Full Moon if you want peace and quiet. At other times though, Ko Pha-Ngan can be seriously tranquil and its east coast is full of secluded

OZEROV ALEXANDER/SHUTTERSTOCK ©

lengths of sand and sheltered coves. Ko Tao is similarly fringed with some lovely beaches.

Best Beaches

Hat Thong Reng Small but serene and perfectly formed. (p115)

Ao Tanot On the far side of Ko Tao, with excellent snorkelling. (p130)

Ao Phang Ka A vast flatland of sand when the tide is out. (p96)

Hat Khuat Fine Ko Tao choice for swimming or snorkelling. (p107)

Hat Thian Isolated Ko Tao beach on the east coast. (p107)

Best for Sunsets

Secret Beach Idyllic views from Ko Pha-Ngan's west coast. (p118)

Ao Phang Ka Sheltered away in the southwest of Ko Samui. (p96)

Na Thon Beach Full-on west coast Ko Samui visuals. (p96)

Best for Sunrises

Hat Thong Reng Lovely at any time of day, but even better at sunrise. (p115)

Ao Tanot Throw down your towel and enjoy. (p130)

Chaweng Beach Square on to the rising sun. (p54)

Hat Ban Hua Thanon Lovely early morning colours for Instagrammers. (p68)

Most Secluded Beaches

Hat Thong Reng Little-visited parcel of sand on Ko Pha-Ngan. (p115)

Laem Thian Beach Remote, sheltered and strewn with white sand, on Ko Tao. (p134)

Ao Phang Ka Way down in the southeast of Ko Samui. (p96)

Hat Yao (East) Remote white-sand beach on Ko Pha-Ngan's southeast coast. (p107)

Hat Khuat Sheltered away on the north coast of Ko Pha-Ngan. (p107)

Hat Wai Nam Super-secluded, on Ko Pha-Ngan. (p107)

Entertainment

Probably because Ko Samui and the other islands of the Lower Gulf have such a wealth of natural beach-side activities and natural allure, the entertainment industry is not well developed. Most entertainment is provided by ladyboy cabaret acts on Ko Samui and Ko Tao, but you can find live music in numerous bars and pubs and fire shows every night on the islands' beaches.

Ladyboy Cabaret

The signature entertainment form on Ko Samui and Ko Tao are *gà·teu·i* (ladyboys; also spelt *kàthoey*), generally cross-dressers or transgendered people, who assume a flamboyant feminine persona. Ladyboy cabarets flourish in Chaweng and Sairee Village on Ko Pha-Ngan and feature feather boas and synchronised stage shows with varying degrees of total cheesiness.

Fire Shows

Entrancing and hypnotising fire shows start whirling soon after sundown on the beaches of all three islands, usually in the vicinity of beach bars such as Coco Tam's (p43) and Fizz (p127).

Live Music

Chaweng is the hub of live music on Ko Samui with live acts serenading punters every night of the week. Most music is of the anthem singalong variety in pubs, bars and open-air venues, such as Hard Rock Cafe (p51) and Saw-asdee Bar (p51). For local pop music, try the Bang Kao Walking Street down on the Ko Samui south coast, where Buffalo Baby (p72) can be found.

Cinema

On an island not strong on entertainment outside of the full moon, Moonlight Cinema (p123) on the outskirts of Thong Sala on Ko Pha-Ngan is a terrific venture, with a big screen in a garden/jungle setting, which concocts a highly relaxing and enjoyable experience.

STEPHEN J. BOITANO/GETTY IMAGES ©

Best Entertainment

Paris Follies Cabaret The top ladyboy show in Chaweng. (p60)

Queen's Cabaret Ko Tao's top entertainment experience and ladyboy extravaganza. (p138)

Moonlight Cinema Highly relaxing and fun movie experience in a Ko Pha-Ngan garden. (p123)

Sawasdee Bar Relaxing choice for alfresco sounds at the heart of Chaweng. (p51)

Best Shows

Paris Follies Cabaret Dazzling and fun ladyboy cabaret on the Chaweng strip. (p60)

Queen's Cabaret Ko Tao's definitive entertainment experience. (p138)

Best for Live Music

Sawasdee Bar Fun, alfresco bar right in the middle of Chaweng. (p51)

Samui Shamrock Irish Pub Live sounds every night. (p75)

Buffalo Baby For local bands on Saturday nights on Ko Samui. (p72)

Diving & Snorkelling

If you've never been diving before, Ko Tao is the place in Thailand to lose your scuba virginity: the waters are crystal clear, there are loads of neon reefs and temperatures are bathwater warm. If you're short on time and don't want to leave Samui, there are plenty of operators who will take you to the same dive sites (for a greater fee, of course).

Dive Schools

On Ko Tao, diving prices are somewhat standardised across the island, so there's no need to spend your time hunting around for the best deal. Most dive schools will hook you up with cheap or even free accommodation. Almost all scuba centres offer gratis fan rooms for anyone doing beginner coursework. Expect large crowds and booked-out beds throughout December, January, June, July and August, and a monthly glut of wannabe divers after every Full Moon Party on Ko Pha-Ngan.

Freediving

Over the last couple of years freediving (exploring the sea using breath-holding techniques rather than scuba gear) has grown massively in popularity, attracting those without any diving experience, as well as those with considerable scuba diving mileage under their belts, and all points in between. Schools can be found on Ko Pha-Ngan and Ko Tao. On Ko Tao, freediving prices are pretty much standardised across the island – a 2½-day SSI beginner course will set you back 5500B.

Snorkelling

On Ko Tao and Ko Pha-Ngan, the small bungalow operations often offer equipment rental for between 100B and 200B per day. Snorkelling tours on Ko Tao range from 500B to 800B (usually including gear, lunch and a guide/boat captain) and stop at various snorkelling hot spots around the island.

THINK4PHOTOP/SHUTTERSTOCK ©

Best Diving Schools

Crystal Dive (www.crystal dive.com) High-quality instructors and intimate classes; Ko Tao-based.

The Life Aquatic (www. thelifeaquatic.asia) Run by a very able and experienced team out of Bo Phut.

Scuba Junction (www. scubajunctiondiving.com) Outgoing and professional team on Ko Tao.

Calypso Diving (www. calypso-diving-kohtao.de) Based in Ao Tanot on the east coast of Ko Tao.

Best Freediving Schools

Apnea Total (www.apnea total.com) Very professional, welcoming and able; on Ko Tao.

Blue Immersion (www. blue-immersion.com) For total newbies, or born-again dolphins; on Ko Tao.

Apnea Koh Pha Ngan (www.apneakohphangan. com) Knowledgeable and efficient.

Best Snorkelling

Ao Tanot Crystal-clear waters on the east of Ko Tao. (p130)

Hin Wong Splendidly clear waters with superb underwater visuals, on Ko Tao. (p134)

Ang Thong Marine National Park Explore the waters around this beautiful cluster of islands. (p102)

Hat Khuat Lovely waters off the north of Ko Pha-Ngan. (p107)

Lighthouse Bay Great for diving and snorkelling, on Ko Tao. (p139)

Top Tips

○ If you're not in a rush, check out a couple of diving schools before making a decision.

○ Ko Tao fills up straight after the Full Moon Party on Ko Pha-Ngan, so choose your time wisely: the days just before and during the full moon are much quieter.

Temples

The islands may draw visitors to their silken sands, moonlit parties and coconut palms, but religious life is a rewarding aspect that engages travellers with local beliefs and worship. Temples are mainly Buddhist, but some Chinese temples are also more Taoist in nature, and you can find a mosque and a church or two.

DMITRY CHULOV/GETTY IMAGES ©

Best *Wát*

Wat Plai Laem The best-looking temple on Ko Samui, perched photogenically over a lake. (p34)

Wat Racha Thammaram With a striking red hall fashioned from clay. (p68)

Wat Khunaram Home to a meditatively seated mummified monk. (p69)

Laem Saw Pagoda Right by the sea on the south shore of Ko Samui, with delightful views. (p79)

Wat Samret Tranquil and reclusive temple in the south of Ko Samui. (p68)

Wat Phra Yai Ko Samui's most photogenic temple, with fine views at sunset. (p40)

Best Chinese Temples

Wat Plai Laem Gorgeous collection of huge and colourful Chinese statues. (p34)

Hainan Temple Abundantly colourful temple on the west coast of Ko Samui. (p98)

Guanyin Temple Extravagant temple to the Buddhist Goddess of Compassion. (p119)

Statue of Guanyu With a temple dedicated to the Chinese general, near Ban Hua Thanon. (p68)

Mae Nam Chinese Temple Diminutive and very colourful beach-side temple at the heart of Mae Nam. (p83)

Best Non-Buddhist Shrines

Ko Samui Central Mosque Imposing green mosque in the Muslim village of Ban Hua Thanon. (p68)

St Anna Catholic Church Small and retiring house of worship near Na Thon. (p96)

Hainan Temple Chinese multi-faith temple and guildhall. (p98)

Top Tips

○ Be respectful to monks and worshippers.

○ Visit temples early in the morning or late in the afternoon for the most photogenic light.

For Kids

The beaches of the Lower Gulf islands make a terrific playground for kids of all ages. For older children, Chaweng is certainly the most entertaining, but for young kids, pretty much any beach will do. If they tire of the sand, plenty of other fun diversions take up the slack.

LEVRANII/GETTY IMAGES ©

Best Water Activities

Sea Walking (www.seawalkingsamui.com) Strolling along the seafloor, for kids above the age of seven.

Red Baron Take the family out on a day-long cruise. (p39)

Wake Up Wakeboarding, wakeskating and waterskiing – ideal for teens. (p119)

Apnea Total (www.apneatotal.com) Kids can join the Junior Freediving course.

Coco Splash Waterpark Waterslide galore. (p71)

Best Landlubber Activities

Football Golf Fun hybrid for groups of tots and teens on Ko Samui. (p40)

Flying Trapeze Adventures Prepare your kids for the circus on Ko Tao. (p135)

Goodtime Adventures Rock-climbing, abseiling, cliff-jumping and more, on Ko Tao. (p135)

Ko Tao Leisure Park Bowling, minigolf, ping pong and other activities. (p134)

Best for Teenagers

Lamai Muay Thai Camp Sharpen up those self-defence skills and get super fit. (p77)

Ko Tao Gym & Fitness Fully equipped gym on Ko Tao. (p136)

Monsoon Gym & Fight Club Ko Tao–based fight school. (p136)

Moonlight Cinema Fun, big-screen movie house in a jungle setting. (p123)

Roctopus Dive Taking youngsters and teens into the world of diving on Ko Tao. (p134)

Top Tips

○ Bring tons of sun cream with you: it's expensive at the pharmacies on all the islands.

○ If you bring a stroller, make it a foldaway umbrella version, as pavements are crowded and curb cutaways rare.

Four Perfect Days

Day 1

NETFALLS REMY MUSSER/SHUTTERSTOCK ©

Start early to photograph the sun lifting from the sea off **Chaweng Beach** (p54) or grab a sunrise breakfast at **Page** (p56). Head to **Wat Plai Laem** (p34) to see the staggering multi-armed statue of Kuan Im.

After a seafood lunch at **Sale-fino** (p40), explore the lanes of **Fisherman's Village** (p36), pop into shops such as **Baan Ngurn** (p46), and chill out in a comfy seat at **Karma Sutra** (p41). Relax on the beach and enjoy the views to Ko Pha-Ngan.

As the sun sets, make it **Coco Tam's** (p43) for a coconut milkshake with gorgeous sea vistas, and later, dine at **Barracuda** (p41) or **2 Fishes** (p40). Head back to Chaweng to gauge its full-on pulsing evening character.

Day 2

FREYA19/GETTY IMAGES ©

Zip down to admire the impressive **Lad Koh Viewpoint** (p54), followed by a long breakfast at **La Fabrique** (p73) in Lamai. Wander **Lamai Beach** (p63) with its sapphire sea, then pay your respects at the Buddhist temples of **Wat Racha Thammaram** (p68), **Wat Khunaram** (p69) or **Wat Samret** (p68).

Dr Frogs (p55) or **The Dining Room** (p74) make great lunch options, then take a dip in the magnificent (but chilly) rock pool at **Na Muang Waterfall** (p64).

Return to Lamai for afternoon drinks, and ensconce yourself at a beachside restaurant such as **Black Pearl** (p73) or **Radiance** (p74) to pass the evening watching the sea and the sand turn silver in the twilight.

Day 3

MARABELO/GETTY IMAGES ©

Consider a trip to **Ang Thong Marine National Park** (p102) or hop aboard a scooter/bike and go via **Ban Hua Thanon** (p79), stopping to explore its market street and beach. Nip to the pagoda of **Laem Saw** (p69) for gorgeous views, and to the bay of **Ao Thong Krut** (p79). Consider a long-tail boat trip to a nearby island.

After lunch at **Hemingway's on the Beach** (p79), head to the lovely crowd-free bay of **Ao Phang Ka** (p96). Make your way up the west coast for sunset at **Air Bar** (p99), a perfect sundown vantage point.

Enjoy a long dinner at **Five Islands** (p98) or **Phootawan Restaurant** (p98). Bring your day to a chilled-out conclusion with an indulgent spa at **Four Seasons Koh Samui** (p143).

Day 4

ANTON EINE/EYEEM/GETTY IMAGES ©

Get up bright and early to walk along the sands of quiet **Mae Nam Beach** (p82), before appreciating the vibrant colours of the **Mae Nam Chinese Temple** (p83). Explore China Town and around before an early lunch at **Fish Restaurant** (p86) or **John's Garden Restaurant** (p87).

Trek (or scooter part-way) to the **Mae Nam Viewpoint** (p83) and **Tan Rua Waterfall** (p91), before winding up the switchbacks to the **View Top** (p91). Admire the panoramas before returning to Mae Nam.

If it's getting close to sunset, try stylish **Woobar** (p44) for drinks, or pop into **Chez Isa** (p44) for ravishing sunset views. For dinner, head to **Farmer** (p87) or **Pepenero** (p86).

Need to Know

For detailed information, see Survival Guide (p140)

Currency
Thai baht (B)

Language
Thai

Visas
Citizens of 62 countries, including Australia, Canada, New Zealand, South Africa, the UK and the USA can stay in Thailand for 30 days without a visa.

Money
ATMs widely available. Credit cards accepted in most hotels and restaurants.

Mobile Phones
Thailand is on the GSM network. Providers include AIS and DTAC.

Time
Indochina Time Zone (GMT/UTC plus seven hours)

Tipping
Tipping is not generally expected, though it is certainly appreciated. Check, however, if a 10% service charge has been added to your bill.

Daily Budget

Budget: less than 800B
Basic fan bungalow or dorm: 200–600B
Market/street-stall meal: 40–100B
Bottle of beer: 80B
Transport: 50–100B

Midrange: 1000–3000B
Flashpacker guesthouse or midrange hotel room: 800–2000B
Western or seafood meal: 200–400B
Organised tour or activity: 800–1500B
Scooter or motorbike hire: 150–300B

Top End: more than 3000B
Boutique villa or hotel room: 3000B and above
Fine dining: 400–1000B
Private tour: 2500B
Car hire: from 800B

Advance Planning

Three months before Check your vaccinations are up to date. Book accommodation at sell-out boutique properties.

One month before Book accommodation for the Full Moon Party on Ko Pha-Ngan, if going.

A few days before Check the weather on the Ko Samui website (www.kosamui.com/weather).

Arriving in Ko Samui

✈ From Samui International Airport

Taxis run to all points of the island. Typical fares include: Chaweng 500B, Bo Phut 500B, Mae Nam 700B, Lamai 800B, Ban Hua Thanon 1000B and Na Thon 1000B.

⛴ From Na Thon Port

Taxis run to all points of the island. Typical fares include Chaweng 1000B, Mae Nam 700B and Bo Phut 800B. *Sŏrng·tǎa·ou* (pick-up minibuses) also leave periodically from near Na Thon pier to points around the ring road – it's 100B to Chaweng.

Getting Around

Note that once you're in the Ko Samui sticks, you'll see signs everywhere for this or that bar, this or that restaurant or hotel, with a distance inscribed. As a rough guide, 300m on these signs equals 1km.

ᨺᨺ Bicycle

The main roads are well surfaced, but watch out for bad driving. Ask at the ubiquitous scooter rental shops about bike rental.

⛴ Boat

The island has extensive boat links to Ko Samui, Ko Pha-Ngan, Ko Tao and Donsak Pier (for Surat Thani); it's the only way to get around between the islands.

🚗 Car & Motorcycle

You can rent motorcycles/scooters from almost every resort (scooters are 150B to 200B per day; for longer periods, negotiate a better rate). Wear a helmet and drive slowly. Car rental is widely available.

🚐 Sŏrng·tǎa·ou

These pick-up minibuses run regularly during daylight hours. Drivers love to try to overcharge you, so ask a third party for current rates. It's about 50B to travel between beaches, and no more than 100B to travel halfway across the island.

🚗 Taxi

Prices are now more standardised across the islands (though ridiculously inflated compared to Bangkok). Taxis typically charge around 500B for an airport transfer.

Ko Samui Regions

Diving off Ko Tao

West Coast Sunsets

Ao Tanot

Ko Tao (p125)
While Ko Tao is the country cousin to Samui's 'big city', it can hold its own against its flamboyant neighbours thanks to a reputation as a dive mecca.

Mae Nam & the North Coast (p81)
Mae Nam offers the right balance of Thai necessities and beach distractions, with the north coast's most striking beach.

Na Thon & the West (p93)
Na Thon is the working side of the island, but further south 'civilisation' soon disappears and villages spring up amid coconut plantations.

Trat
(325km)

Ko Pha-Ngan (p105)
The perfect island –
carved into sandy coves
with offshore reefs on
the west coast and with
a thick jungle crown –
there is something for
everyone.

**Bo Phut & the
Northeast (p33)**
Samui's 'alternative'
coast, where
commercial
development is more
subdued and crowds
are more discerning and
worldly than on the east
coast.

*Ko Pha-Ngan's
Hidden Beaches*
◉

• Thong
Sala

*Full Moon
Party*
◉

Hat Chaweng (p49)
With its international-
style resorts, Chaweng's
commercial strip is a
little Bangkok by the sea
that wakes up at noon
and parties well into the
next day.

*Around
Mae Nam*
◉   *Wat Plai
Laem*
◉

*Fisherman's
Village*
◉

*Samui
International
Airport*

◉ *Na Muang
Falls*

**Hat Lamai & the
Southeast (p63)**
The most traditional
part of the island, with
glimpses of Samui's
past as the 'coconut
island' and the greatest
concentration of
nonbeach attractions.

Explore
Ko Samui

Fire twirling on the beach MICHAEL LEPETIT/GETTY IMAGES ©

Explore ◉

Bo Phut & the Northeast

Bo Phut and the northeast of the island have far less congestion than the more crowded east coast, while the beaches are more tranquil and sunset vantage points await. Though it can get packed, Fisherman's Village strikes a balance between commercialism and the traditional charm of an old fishing town, while supplying some of the best food on the island.

Visit Bo Phut Beach (p39) in the early morning to take advantage of the soft light and consider breakfast at the languorous and comfy Karma Sutra (p41). You can explore Fisherman's Village (p36) at any time of the day – although the morning sees the neighbourhood less visited and sets you up for lunch, while late afternoon provides an abundant choice of dinner options. Late afternoon is also the best time to explore the Buddhist temples here – Wat Plai Laem (p34) is the more celebrated, but sibling Wat Phra Yai (p40) is the more photogenic. For a superb vantage point for the setting sun pop into Chez Isa (p44) next door or drop by Coco Tam's (p43) for a cocktail as the sun slides behind the headland to the west.

Getting There & Around

Bo Phut is easily reached by scooter, *sŏrng·tăa·ou* (pick-up minibus), taxi or on foot. Boats to Ko Pha-Ngan and Ko Tao leave from the Big Buddha Beach pier.

Po Phut & the Northeast Map on p38

Wat Phra Yai (p40), Ko Samui LUKAKIKINA/SHUTTERSTOCK ©

Top Experience
Wat Plai Laem

Ko Samui's most colourful, charming and sceni-
cally situated temple can be discovered in the
northeast of the island, not too far from Wat
Phra Yai. It's a recently built and rather unusual
Thai- and Chinese-style Buddhist temple dedi-
cated to Guanyin (the bodhisattva of mercy and
compassion) and the Budai Buddha, built on a
lake and reflected in clear waters.

◉ MAP P38, E2

admission free

☉ dawn-dusk

Guanyin (Kwan Im)

The most arresting sight in the temple grounds, the vibrantly painted Buddhist bodhisattva of compassion has 18 arms, arrayed in a magnificent fan around and above her body. Seated on a lotus pedestal around which a dragon coils and dispensing endless mercy to those who pray to her, the statue is accessed along a tiled bridge, her form reflected in the still water.

Despite the modern nature of the temple, the goddess exudes a powerful sense of sympathy. By the green head of the dragon, below her, a constellation of small effigies of the goddess are gathered. Her image, framed against the blue skies of Ko Samui, make for excellent photo ops, especially at the end of the day as the lowering sun casts a warm glow over the deity. This type of Guanyin is commonly known as a 'thousand-arm Guanyin', even though she does not sport that many limbs.

Budai Buddha

Seated upon a lotus pedestal, the jovial, bald and laughing Budai Buddha is considered to be a manifestation of the Maitreya, or future, Buddha. The term Budai (cloth bag) points to the fabric sack he holds in one hand, which contains his few possessions. In Chinese temples, Budai (also called Milefo) is typically found at the immediate entrance to the compound, always smiling and welcoming worshippers.

Main Hall

Between Guanyin and Budai Buddha, the main saffron-tiled and gold decorated Thai-style hall also finds itself on an island in the lake, a situation that amplifies its contours through reflections upon the water's surface. The structure is accessed along a bridge and up steps with balustrades topped with colourful dragons. The ceiling of the hall is a beautiful confection of pomegranate, gold, pink and blue.

★ **Top Tips**

○ Visit either in the early morning or towards dusk, when the most photogenic light is cast over the statues.

○ Also visit the nearby Wat Phra Yai (Big Buddha Temple) and visit in the late afternoon to see the sun set from Wat Phra Yai.

✕ **Take a Break**

Not far from Wat Plai Laem, near the entrance to Wat Phra Yai, Chez Isa (p44) is a fine choice for comfort, scenic views over the water, excellent coffee and some breathtaking sunsets.

Getting There

Scooter Along the 4171 and look for the turning around 600m from the road to Wat Phra Yai (Temple of the Big Buddha).

Top Experience
Fisherman's Village

This concentration of narrow Chinese shop-houses has been transformed into trendy (and often midrange) boutique hotels, eateries, cafes and bars. The accompanying beach, particularly the eastern part, is slim and coarse but becomes whiter and lusher further west. The combination of pretty sands and gussied-up old village is a winner, but it can get busy during peak season. In the low season, it's lovely, quiet and elbow free.

MAP P38, B1

Alleys & Lanes

The lanes and side streets of Fisherman's Village afford a charming half-day wander, punctuated with coffees, snacks, a full-blown meal at one of the many restaurants and a stroll on the beach. Wandering to your heart's content is the name of the game, popping into shops to load up with souvenirs or sinking a latte and having a breather in a cafe while watching the world go by.

Walking Street

Every Friday night, this busy and colourful market (p46) transforms Fisherman's Village into a forest of sharp elbows, stalls, steaming street food, handicrafts, T-shirts and cheap cocktails. The neighbourhood is at its perkiest, so it can get hectic, but it's also a super fun time to pitch up and see Fisherman's Village at its most colourful and vibrant. Snacks galore await.

Coco Tam's

No visit to Fisherman's Village remains complete without a super-smooth coconut shake, or something with more bite, at Coco Tam's (p43) beach bar. The idyllic time is at sundown as twilight settles over the sand – sit yourself down in one of its swings bar-side or collapse into a beanbag on the beach.

The Wharf

Stuffed with shops, The Wharf has high prices but there's heaps of quality choice, and the lower crowd density than the sometimes crowded alleys makes it a quiet diversion. It's also home to the superb restaurant, Barracuda (p41), and a great **dive shop** (☑086 030 0286; www.thelifeaquatic.asia).

★ Top Tip

○ Head to Fisherman's Village on Friday night when Fisherman's Village Walking Street (p46) is on for the best atmosphere and excellent photo ops.

✕ Take a Break

Coco Tam's (p43) is at hand for a superb break from schlepping.

For a sensational evening meal, make it Barracuda (p41), a short stroll from the sea.

Getting There

Sŏrng·tăa·ou (pick-up minibus) Ply the ring road around the island.

Taxi From Chaweng about 500B.

Scooter Along the 4169.

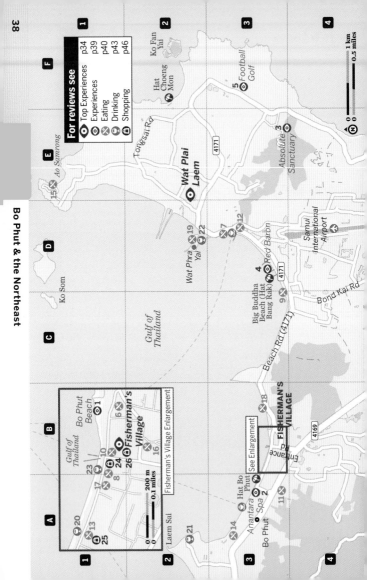

Bo Phut & the Northeast

Gulf of Thailand

For reviews see
Top Experiences	p34
Experiences	p39
Eating	p40
Drinking	p43
Shopping	p46

Ao Samrong

Ko Som

Ko Fan Yai

Hat Choeng Mon

Tongsai Rd

Wat Plai Laem

Football
Golf

5

Absolute Sanctuary

3

4171

Wat Phra Yai 19 22 7 12

Red Baron

Big Buddha Beach (Hat Bang Rak)
4

9

4171

Samui International Airport

Bond Kai Rd

Beach Rd (4171)

18

FISHERMAN'S VILLAGE

See Enlargement

Entrance Rd

4169

11

Anantara Spa 2

Bo Phut

Hat Bo Phut

14

21

Laem Sai

Fisherman's Village Enlargement

Bo Phut Beach

1

6

16

Fisherman's Village

10 24 26

23 17 8

20 13 25

Gulf of Thailand

0   200 m
0   0.1 miles

0   1 km
0   0.5 miles

Experiences

Bo Phut Beach

BEACH

1 ⊙ MAP P38, B1

Rather coarse and shelly, Bo Phut's beach inclines rather steeply into cloudy water, but the views are scenic to Ko Pha-Ngan, an island that acts as a buffer to seasonal winds and calms the waters.

Anantara Spa

SPA

2 ⊙ MAP P38, A3

Anantara Spa provides serene pampering in a sublime setting of lush tropical foliage, with a soft-edged focus on Ayurvedic treatments. (📞077 428300; www.anantara.com/en/bophut-koh-samui/spa; Bo Phut; ⊙10am-10pm)

Absolute Sanctuary

YOGA, SPA

3 ⊙ MAP P38, E3

Detox, spa, yoga, Pilates, fasting, lifestyle and nutrition packages, in an alluring Moroccan-inspired setting. (📞077 601190; www.absolutesanctuary.com; Choeng Mon)

Red Baron

CRUISE

4 ⊙ MAP P38, D3

With day-long cruises around Ko Samui (9.30am Tuesday), brunch trips to Ko Pha-Ngan (11am Wednesday and Sunday), sunset dinner cruises to Ko Som (4.30pm Monday and Friday) and journeys over the waves to Ang Thong Marine Park (8.30am Thursday), *Red Baron* is a traditional and very popular sailing junk moored at Bangrak. Meals and drinks

Anantara Spa

Wat Phra Yai

On a rocky island linked to the coastline by a causeway towards the northeastern tip of Ko Samui, **Wat Phra Yai** (Temple of the Big Buddha; admission free; ⏰dawn-dusk) was erected in 1972. The modern Buddha (sitting in the Mara posture) stands 15m high, alluringly framed against the tropical sky and sea. The temple is most animated during religious festivals such as Songkran and Loy Kratong. Excellent views range from the top, especially at sunset, which is a great time to walk around the rocky coastline behind the temple. Wear appropriate clothes when visiting the temple (see p45).

provided. Private charters also available. (contact@redbaron-samui. com; Hat Bang Rak; from 2500B)

Football Golf

GOLF

5 MAP P38, F3

A curious hybrid called 'football golf' where you 'putt' your football into a rubbish-bin-sized hole. It's great for the kids and each game comes with a complimentary soft drink. It's not a solo game, so make sure you're a group and go either soon after it opens or wait till late afternoon, when it's cooler. (☎089 771 7498; www.samuifootballgolf.com;

Hat Choeng Mon; adult/child 730/ 350B; ⏰9am-6.30pm)

Eating

The Hut

THAI $

6 🍴 MAP P38, B1

Basic, reasonably priced Thai specialities share space with more expensive fresh seafood and Western treats, but the dozen or so tables fill fast so get here early or late if you don't want to wait. If you're a fisherman this is the place to get your own catch cooked up. Negative point: staff can be very surly. (☎087 278 1536; Fisherman's Village; mains 60-550B; ⏰1-10pm)

Salefino

MEDITERRANEAN $$

7 🍴 MAP P38, D3

This new restaurant (sister establishment of Pepenero, p86) serves delightful seafood, pasta and tapas dishes with a strong tilt towards Italian. There's a fine selection of wines and a lovely setting by the sea, all viewed from a rustic chic interior; dinner is particularly charming, with sunset. (☎091 825 2190; www.salefinosamui. com; Hat Bang Rak; ⏰1-3pm & 5-9pm Mon-Fri, 5-10.30pm Sat)

2 Fishes

ITALIAN $$

8 🍴 MAP P38, B1

This new, competent Italian restaurant is a breath of fresh air, with a neat personality and a tasty, appetising menu. Portions are not large, but service is prompt, overseen by the welcoming and polite owner Leandro. (☎077 901009; www.2fishessamui.com; Fisherman's Village; mains from 250B; ⏱5.30pm-late Tue-Sun)

Antica Locanda ITALIAN $$

 9 MAP P38, C3

This friendly trattoria has pressed white tablecloths and caskets of Italian wine. Try the *vongole alla marinara* (clams in white wine), but also consider the succulent specials of the day. (☎077 245163; www.anticasamui.com; Hat Bang Rak; mains from 240B; ⏱1-11pm; 📶)

Karma Sutra INTERNATIONAL $$

10 MAP P38, B1

A hip haze of purples and pillows, beanbags and low tables, this comfy chow spot straddles the crossroads heart of the village, dishing up very good international and Thai eats, with outdoor seating by the people-watching wayside. (Fisherman's Village; mains 180-700B; ⏱7.30am-1am; 📶)

69 FUSION $$

11 MAP P38, A3

The simply roaring roadside setting puts it on the wrong side of the tracks, and the dated, eclectic decor is limp and tired; that said, almost unanimous rave reviews for its creative twists on Thai favourites make this a really popular choice, though not all dishes dazzle. (☎081 978 1945; Route 4169,

near Fisherman's Village; mains from 150B; ⏱1-10pm; 📶)

Catcantoo INTERNATIONAL $$

12 MAP P38, D3

Enjoy excellent value breakfasts in the morning, succulent ribs at noon, or shooting pool later in the day. (Hat Bang Rak; mains 90-350B; ⏱10am-1am)

Barracuda MEDITERRANEAN $$$

13 MAP P38, A1

Abounding in alluring Mediterranean culinary inflections, but only open come evening, Barracuda is one of the island's best dining options. The romantic and seductive night-time environment is almost as delightful as the menu: expect to be charmed and well fed on a diet of seared scallops, yellowfin tuna, rack of lamb, Norwegian salmon, delectable pasta dishes and fine service. (☎077 430003; www.barracuda-restaurant.com; The Wharf, Fisherman's Village; mains from 575B; ⏱6-11pm)

Zazen Restaurant FUSION $$$

14 MAP P38, A3

This superb romantic dining experience at the **Zazen Resort** (www.samuizazen.com; Bo Phut; r ฿6160-17,200B; ❄@📶❌) comes complete with ocean views, dim candle lighting and soft music. Thai dancers animate things on Thursday and Sunday nights from 8pm. Reservations recommended.

Twilight Cocktails at Coco Tam's

Stop by Coco Tam's on the beach near the Wharf at Fisherman's Village for cocktails at twilight and watch the sun setting behind the headland. Aim for one of the bar-side swings, or collapse into a beanbag and let the twilight atmosphere work its magic, with the sound of the surf lapping gently on the shore as the sea turns platinum and fire dancers get to work.

(☑077 425085, 098 015 8986; dishes 540-900B, set menu from 1300B; ⏱lunch & dinner)

Dining on the Rocks

FUSION $$$

15 ✖ MAP P38, E1

At the isolated **Six Senses Samui** (www.sixsenses.com/resorts/samui/destination; bungalows from 15,625B; ❄@🛜🏊), the island's ultimate dining experience takes place on nine cantilevered verandahs yawning over the gulf. After sunset (and wine), guests feel like they're dining on a barge set adrift on a starlit sea. Each dish on the set menu is the brainchild of cooks experimenting with taste, texture and temperature. (☑077 245678; www.sixsenses.com/resorts/samui/dining; Choeng Mon; set menus from 2800B; ⏱5-10pm)

Chez François

FRENCH $$$

16 ✖ MAP P38, B2

With no à la carte menu, but a reputation for outstanding cuisine that has sent waves across the culinary map of Ko Samui, Chez François serves a three-course surprise meal. Book ahead – and if you're only on Ko Samui for a few days, book early to get a table. It's tiny (and cash only).

Chez François is hidden away behind a wooden door near a pharmacy. (☑096 071 1800; www.facebook.com/chezporte; 33/2 Mu 1, Fisherman's Village; set meal 1700-1950B; ⏱6-11pm Tue-Sat)

Shack Bar & Grill

STEAK $$$

17 ✖ MAP P38, A1

The Shack imports the finest cuts of meat from Australia and slathers them in a rainbow of tasty sauces from red wine to blue cheese. Booth seating and jazz over the speakers give the joint a distinctly Western vibe, though you'll find all types of diners coming here to splurge. (☑087 264 6994; www.theshackgrillsamui.com; Fisherman's Village; mains 450-800B; ⏱5.30-11pm)

Ninja Crepes

THAI $

18 MAP P38, B3

The owners of this great place were recently turfed out of their lucrative Chaweng restaurant, but the pay-off is fine sea views; the location sees less custom, but that makes it quieter too. Expect Thai seafood, curries, crêpes, soups and sticky desserts. (4171 Beach Rd, Bo Phut; mains from 80B; 9am-9pm)

Leonardo Gelateria Italiana

GELATO $$

19 MAP P38, D2

This small gelateria is not cheap – it's 150B for one cup of ice cream or sorbet – but there's a tempting range of 25 flavours and it stands out among the disappointing selection of eateries at Wat Phra Yai. Choose from lime, mango, tiramisu, pistachio, coconut, blackberry, passion fruit, black chocolate and more. (092 847 7385; Wat Phra Yai; from 150B; 9am-6pm)

Drinking

Coco Tam's

BAR

20 MAP P38, A1

Grab a swing at the bar or plop yourself on a beanbag on the sand, order a giant cocktail served in a jar and take a toke on a shisha (water pipe; 500B). It's a bit pricey, but this boho, beach-bum-chic spot oozes relaxation, it's lovely when the sun goes down and the coconut milkshakes are to die for. Fire dancers perform most nights. (Fisherman's Village; 1pm-1am)

Six Senses Samui

Woobar BAR

21 MAP P38, A2

With serious wow factor and 270-degree panoramas, the W Retreat's signature lobby bar gives the word 'swish' a whole new meaning, with cushion-clad pods of seating plonked in the middle of an expansive infinity pool that stretches out over the infinite horizon. This is, without doubt, the best place on Samui for sunset cocktails blended with cool music mixes. There's a strong craft beer list too. (077 915999; Bo Phut; 11am-midnight;)

Chez Isa CAFE

22 MAP P38, D2

This small, charming and colourful cafe serves no alcohol (as Wat Phra Yai is alongside) and shuts early, but it's a lovely spot to catch the sunset with a mocktail held aloft or relax with a coffee during the day, looking out to sea. There's a range of jewellery for sale too. (082 423 9221; Wat Phra Yai; 9.30am-7pm;)

Billabong Surf Club BAR

23 MAP P38, B1

Solid Billabong's all about Aussie Rules football – it's on the TV and the walls are smothered with signed shirts and memorabilia from Down Undah. Outside, there are great views of Ko Pha-Ngan to go with your hearty portions of ribs, chops and draught beer. (Fisherman's Village; 9am-1am;)

Woobar

LEISA TYLER/GETTY IMAGES ©

Temples & Religious Life

The island is sprinkled with Buddhist temples (*wát*), which can provide the most traditional window to authentic Thai life away from Ko Samui's more manufactured tourist dimension. Remove your shoes if entering temple halls and don't wear over-revealing clothing or swimwear; shirts to the elbow and trousers that go to the knee are expected.

Buddhist Temples

Most temples on the island are Theravada Buddhist, though not all. Wat Plai Laem (p34) is notably a more Mahayana temple, evident in its large statues of bodhisattva (Buddhas-to-be) worshipped across China, Japan and South Korea. As there isn't one prescribed day for worship, temples are always open to worshippers who come to make merit, by lighting incense sticks and offering lotus blossoms before the temple's principal Buddha figure.

Buddhist Symbols & Motifs

Many temples are venerated for revered temple abbots who live or lived there, for their architecture, their history or their setting. Sacred motifs in Buddhist temples include the lotus bud and the lotus flower, which grows from the mud at the bottom of a pond or lake, symbolising perfection emerging from impurity. Many temples on the island also have rows of small *chedi* (stupa) that contain the remains of noted nuns or monks.

Other Temples & Places of Worship

There are several Chinese temples on the island that are more Taoist than Buddhist; the most famous are the Chinese Temple (p83) in Mae Nam and the Hainan Temple (p98) in Na Thon. There's a green mosque (p68) in the Muslim village of Ban Hua Thanon and the St Anna Catholic Church (p96) is near Na Thon on the west of the island.

Away from the temples, you will also see small decorative houses on pedestals with offerings of fruit and incense. These are spirit houses, an animistic tradition that gives a comfortable dwelling place for a site's earthly guardian. You will also notice spirit trees, in which spirits reside, garlanded in bright and colourful ribbons in temples or at the wayside.

Kwan Im
(Buddhist Goddess of Mercy)

The magnificent 18-armed statue of Kwan Im at Wat Plai Laem (p34) reveals a growing interest among Thai people in this bodhisattva that is most associated with the Mahayana Buddhist tradition – a fascination that partly springs from the burgeoning influence on the island of China and the Chinese.

Kwan Im, the Buddhist Goddess of Mercy – or more strictly a bodhisattva (Buddha-to-be), in the Mahayana tradition – shoulders the grief of the world and dispenses mercy and compassion. Her name derives from Guanyin, a Chinese name that is itself a contraction of Guanshiyin, which translates as 'to hear the cries of the world'.

In Sanksrit, she is known as Avalokiteshvara; in Japan, she is called Kannon, while the Cantonese call her Guanyam and her Vietnamese name is Quan Am. In Tibetan Buddhism, her earthly presence manifests itself in the Dalai Lama, and her Tibetan home is the Potala Palace in Lhasa.

Kwan Im also appears in a variety of forms, often with just two arms, but frequently in multi-armed shape.

Shopping

Fisherman's Village
Walking Street   MARKET

 MAP P38, B1

Every Friday night, this busy and colourful Walking Street transforms Fisherman's Village into a forest of sharp elbows, market stalls, street food, handicrafts, T-shirts and cheap cocktails. (⏰5-11pm Fri)

The Wharf   MALL

25 🔒 MAP P38, A1

This upscale mall offers a relaxing open-plan array of shops, boutiques, restaurants and services just a few steps from the beach. Goods for sale include coconut soap, organic creams and oils, embroidered shoes, kid's clothing and jewellery, as well as the usual lacquered coconut shells. Prices are high, but the quality is good and standout options include restaurant Barracuda and dive operation the Life Aquatic. (www.thewharfsamui.com; Fisherman's Village; ⏰11am-11pm)

Baan Ngurn   JEWELLERY

26 🔒 MAP P38, B2

Recently relocated, this small shop has a choice array of finely worked silver bracelets, necklaces and other jewellery. Prices start at around 30B for a pair of earrings to upwards of 8000B, and the owner, Su, is usually open to a bit of haggling. (House of Silver; 📱085 797 9630; www.thaihouseofsilver.com; Fisherman's Village; ⏰10am-10pm Tue-Sun, 5-10pm Mon)

Kwan Im, Wat Plai Laem (p34)

Explore ⊕

Hat Chaweng

Bristling with selfie sticks and an assault course of low-hanging street signs, Chaweng Beach Rd is crowded with souvenir shops, tattoo parlours and pharmacies. If you expected a romantic vision of Ko Samui, this isn't it; but the dining options are superb, the bar/cabaret scene is hopping, the beach isn't bad and it's fun if you want action.

Head to the beach (p54) at dawn to take some ravishing photos of the morning sun over the gulf. Tie it in with breakfast at a beachside restaurant, such as Page (p56). Head south to the Lad Koh Viewpoint (p54) for its stunning views (and a coconut ice cream from the vendor who sets up shop every day). For lunch, stop by a coastal restaurant such as Dr Frogs (p55) or scoot up to Jungle Club (p56) for its ranging views. Spend the afternoon lazing on Chaweng Beach, before exploring the shopping and dining options along Chaweng Beach Rd, before sampling the area's diverse choice of bars.

Getting There & Around

Chaweng is the epicentre of active life on Ko Samui, so all the *sŏrng·tăa·ou* (pick-up minibuses) slew through from all four corners of the island. It's also very near the airport, so is a convenient – if noisy – first port of call. Bangkok Airways has an office in Chaweng and another at the airport. Scooter hire shops are ubiquitous, so this is a good place to rent. Chaweng also has a handy petrol station.

Hat Chaweng Map on p52

Chaweng Beach Road DENNIS COX/ALAMY STOCK PHOTO ©

Walking Tour 🚶

A Night Out in Chaweng

Chaweng Beach Rd at night is a carnival of lights, glitz, action, music and the sounds of a neighbourhood that rarely takes its foot off the pedal. Taking in some of the best known bars of the neighbourhood, embark on this entertaining bar crawl that starts in the heart of the Chaweng action and takes you to the sands of Chaweng Beach, via a cabaret act and live music.

Walk Facts

Start Chaweng Beach Rd

End Chaweng Beach

Length As long as you can keep going

❶ Drink Gallery

Start on a relaxing note with a drink in the stylish, dishy, sophisticated cool of the Drink Gallery (p56) at the Library – a super-neat hotel along Chaweng Beach Rd – where the stunning design is matched by a strong wine and cocktail list. It's in a different league to most of the bars on the road.

❷ Sawasdee Bar

Look out for fun **Sawasdee Bar** (Chaweng Beach Rd; ⏲5pm-midnight) operating from a blue Volkswagen camper outside Central Festival – it's fun and different, with seats dotted about for sedentary enjoyment of the tunes and to people-watch as the crowds move along Chaweng Beach Rd. It sets up Monday to Friday.

❸ Hard Rock Cafe

Walk up Chaweng Beach Rd to pass two hulking new overblown additions to the strip: **Hard Rock Cafe** (☎077 901208; ⏲11.30am-2am), with live music round the back, and Hooters, vying for custom right next door to each other.

❹ Green Mango

You won't miss the cowgirls advertising cheap beers in vast Henry Africa's bar up a side road off the main strip; pop in for a drink and a game of pool or carry on up the side road to the **Green Mango** (☎077 422661; www.thegreenmango club.com; Soi Green Mango), one of Chaweng's most famous

nightspots. If you want peace and quiet, head on to Chaweng Lake, a romantic spot at night.

❺ Paris Follies Cabaret

A short walk north along Chaweng Beach Rd brings you to the Paris Follies Cabaret (p60), unmissable for its tall and amazingly made-up ladyboys handing out fliers to the passing traffic. Chaweng's most famous cabaret show is free to enter, though you need to buy a (pricey) drink.

❻ Legends Bar

Rock-steady Legends Bar (p58) offers Chang beer at a tempting 49B – among the lowest along this strip – with seats out front and sports walls plastered in a medley of rock posters and memorabilia from the golden age of rock. Sit out front to people-watch.

❼ Ark Bar

Head across to Ark Bar (p59) on the beach, with fire jugglers and DJs keeping everyone moving till the early hours. Chill out with a beer or a cocktail and soak up the evening view and atmosphere.

❽ Walk along the Beach

To round off your night, head along the beach – either north or south – listening to music from beachside bars, mixed with the soothing sound of the sea. It's the perfect antidote to the crowds and should remind you why you're on Ko Samui in the first place.

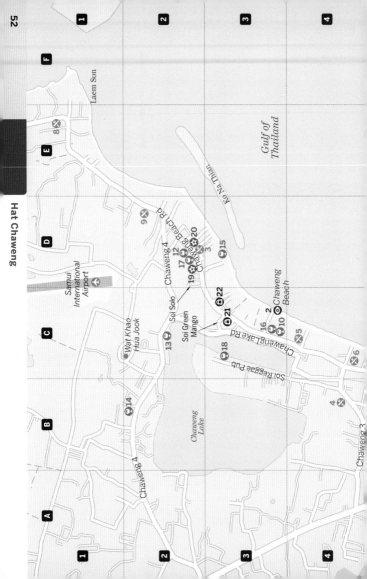

Laem Son

Gulf of
Thailand

Ko Na Thian

Samui
International
Airport

Wat Khao
Hua Jook

Chaweng 4

Soi Solo

Soi Green
Mango

Soi Reggae Pub

Chaweng Lake Rd

Chaweng Beach

Chaweng Lake

Chaweng 4

Chaweng 3

Chaweng 4

Be Beach Rd

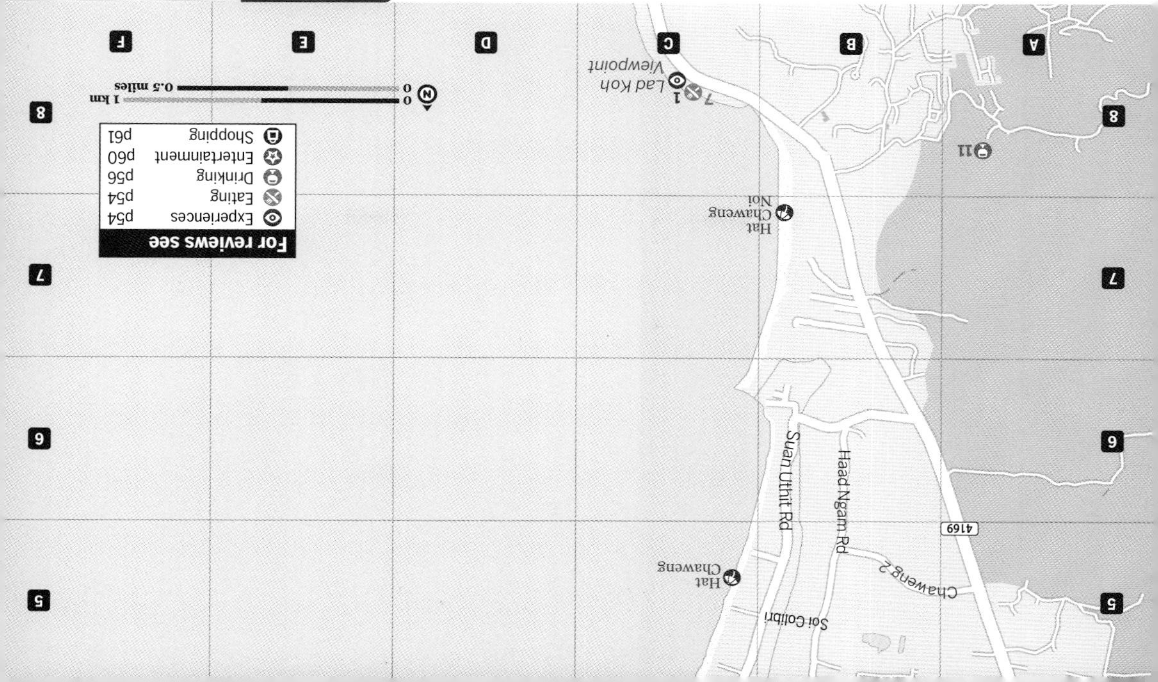

A
B
C
D
E
F
5
6
7
8
Hat Chaweng
Hat Chaweng Noi
Lad Koh Viewpoint
Suan Uthit Rd
Haad Ngam Rd
Soi Colibri
Chaweng 2
4169
1
7
11
For reviews see
Experiences p54
Eating p54
Drinking p56
Entertainment p60
Shopping p61
0 1 km
0 0.5 miles

Experiences

Lad Koh
Viewpoint   VIEWPOINT

1 ◎ MAP P52, C8

This superb viewpoint a short distance south from Dr Frogs at the top of the hill on the way to Lamai looks out onto supreme views of the Gulf of Thailand, with a horizon so long you can just about detect the curvature of the globe. Look out for the coconut-ice-cream wagon that's always here during daylight hours. (off Rte 4169)

Chaweng Beach   BEACH

2 ◎ MAP P52, C3

Lovely for sunrise, by evening this is the busiest and loudest beach on Ko Samui, and during the day it's often hopping too, thanks to the sheer number of resorts and hotels dotted along its length. But it's still a pleasant and pretty enough length of sand and there are loads of dining choices.

Eating

Tuk Tuk
Backpackers   CAFE $

3 ✖ MAP P52, D2

This full-on, no-holds-barred, high-impact, brazen and voluminous saloon-style Western cafe/restaurant/bar on Chaweng Beach Rd does good hangover-cure brekkies, with multiple TV screens, pool tables and all the usual trappings. (📞087 268 2575; Chaweng Beach Rd; mains from 120B; ⊘10am-2am)

Chaweng Beach

Laem Din Market

MARKET $

 4 MAP P52, B4

A busy day market, Laem Din is packed with stalls that sell fresh fruits, vegetables and meats and stock local Thai kitchens. Pick up a kilo of sweet green oranges or wander the stalls trying to spot the ingredients in last night's curry. For dinner, check out the adjacent night market to sample tasty Southern-style fried chicken and curries. (Chaweng; dishes from 35B; 4am-6pm, night market 6pm-2am)

Stacked

STEAK $$

5 MAP P52, C4

All sharp lines, open kitchen/grill, a team of busy and super-efficient staff plus a cracker of a menu, this awesome burger restaurant remains a visual and culinary feast. Burgers and steaks – bursting with flavour – are served up on slate slabs in generous portions. Go with a sizeable hunger as the inclination is to simply keep on ordering. (www.stacked-samui.com; Chaweng Beach Rd; mains from 295B; noon-midnight;)

Hungry Wolf

BURGERS $$

6 MAP P52, C4

With fun, vibrantly designed and catchy murals revolving around British culinary idioms, this neat Polish-run Chaweng restaurant does a good trade in juicy burgers, steaks, ribs, pizza and a whole variety of other delicious fare. It's not big, and attracts considerable

Wat Khao Hua Jook

The golden pagoda of **Wat Khao Hua Jook** (Map p52, C2; Chaweng; admission free; 8am-5pm) sits up Khao Hua Jook Rd on top of the hill north of Chaweng Lake, offering fine views over Chaweng, the air-port and the island. Within the pagoda is a replica of one of Buddha's footprints, an object of veneration to Buddhists from near and far. Look for the turning up the hill off Chaweng Lake Rd, which you can climb on foot or by scooter. You can't miss it at night, when the pagoda is gloriously illuminated and reflected in Chaweng Lake.

custom, but the capable and en-thusiastic owner makes everyone feel at home. (094 408 2243; Chaweng Beach Rd; mains from 220B; 10am-10pm)

Dr Frogs

STEAK $$$

7 MAP P52, C8

Perched atop a rocky overlook, Dr Frogs combines beautiful ocean vistas with delicious international grills, seafood, pasta, pizza and Thai favourites. Delectable steaks and crab cakes, and friendly owners, make it a winner. It's a romantic setting, and for harassed parents there's a kids' playground in the front garden. Live guitar music on Mondays and Wednesdays at 7.30pm. (📞077 448505; www.drfrogssamui.com; Rte 4169; mains from 480B; ⏰7am-11pm)

Page

FUSION $$$

If you can't afford to stay at the ultra-swanky **Library** (📞077 422767; www.thelibrary.co.th; Chaweng Beach Rd; studio/ste incl breakfast from 11,900/13,600B; ❄ @ 🛜 🏊), have a meal at its beachside restaurant instead (see 2 🔵 Map p52, C3). It's not cheap, but lunch is a bit more casual and affordable, although you'll miss the designer lighting in the evening. Sunrise breakfasts are lovely. (www.thelibrarysamui.com/the-page; dishes 300-1650B; ⏰7am-midnight; 🛜)

Larder

EUROPEAN $$$

8 🍴 MAP P52, E1

This restaurant/bar/gastropub pulls out the stops in an invigorating menu of classic fare in a relaxing and tasteful setting, supported by a strong selection of wines and zesty cocktails. It's a winning formula, with dishes ranging from slow-cooked lamb spare ribs to fish and chips. (📞077 601259; www.thelardersamui.com; Chaweng Beach Rd; mains 300-820B; ⏰noon-11pm Mon-Sat; 🛜)

Prego

ITALIAN $$$

9 🍴 MAP P52, D2

This zestfully refreshed restaurant with cool lounge and bar zone serves up tantalising Italian cuisine, with a strong selection of vegetarian dishes, backed up by a tempting wine list. Choose from *fettuccine nere ai sapori di mare* (squid ink seafood fettucine), *risotto gamberi* (prawn risotto) and a host of other appetising selections. (www.prego-samui.com; Chaweng Beach Rd; mains 280-860B; ⏰noon-11pm)

Drinking

Drink Gallery

COCKTAIL BAR

10 🍺 MAP P52, C3

Part of the Library hotel, this highly stylish bar along Chaweng Beach Rd has top design and some excellent cocktails. It's a place to be seen in and a place to people-watch from, or just admire the interior artwork while nibbling on tapas-style Thai bites. (Chaweng Beach Rd; www.thelibrary.co.th; ⏰4pm-1am)

Jungle Club

BAR

11 🍺 MAP P52, A8

With knockout views from its high-altitude perch, you'll want to head up and back sober if on a scooter as the approach is very steep, otherwise Jungle Club can arrange pick-up from Chaweng for 400B, or you can get a taxi for a similar fare. (📞081 894 2327; www.jungleclubsamui.com; ⏰9am-9.30pm)

Ko Samui's History, Development & Tourism

Early History

With so little of Samui's early history being written down or recorded, knowledge of the early days of the island largely derives from oral traditional and history, as related and passed down by elders, with the imprecision and forgetting this entails. Samui didn't begin exercising much influence on regional events until the latter half of the 20th century, before which the island was populated, as oral stories attest, by two families originally from Nakhon Si Thammarat, some traders from southern China and Muslims from the Malay peninsula. During this time, the island was still largely isolated from the mainland by an arduous sea journey, while the mountainous terrain and lack of passable roads across the island kept communities apart.

Growing Trade & Infrastructure

The first cash crop was coconuts, as plantations flourished in the interior mountains, which began to bring the island closer to the outside world. Coconut-shipping boats would make the journey between the mainland and the island, kick-starting the need for the development of infrastructure and facilities. In the late 1960s the central government was successfully lobbied to build a road on the island – a construction project that initially relied solely on manual labour but had to import heavy equipment from the mainland to grade high-terrain. The double-lane Ring Rd (Rd 4169) was eventually completed in 1973, running around the island.

Arrival of Tourism

By far the most dramatic event in the island's history was the first foreign tourist foot arriving on Ko Samui's sands, sometime in the early 1970s. Lamai, and later Chaweng, began luring bands of young backpackers with its white sand beaches, easygoing island life and easy access to marijuana. Ko Samui airport was constructed in 1989 and family guesthouses started to go upmarket in search of package tourists, with luxury hotels beginning to appear.

The latest transformation has come with the flood of Chinese tourists, who are leaving their mark on the island, in pretty much the same way that Western visitors of the 1980s and 1990s transformed Ko Samui.

Swimming Hazards

Chaweng and Lamai experience strong currents and rip tides even if the waters look calm: hotels will usually post warnings of swimming hazards and conditions on a beach board or warning flags. If you are caught in a rip tide (a strong surface current heading seaward), it is advised not to fight it and rapidly tire, but instead to swim parallel to the shore to exit the current or float along with it until it dissipates in deeper water and you are deposited.

Pride Bar
GAY & LESBIAN

12 MAP P52, D2

At the heart of Chaweng, this easygoing place attracts a mixed crowd of Thais and foreigners. (☏088 753 2921; Chaweng Beach Rd; ⏰5pm-2am)

Legends Bar
BAR

Located next door to Bar Solo (see 17 Map p52, D2), rollicking Legends bar is aimed at the older crowd, serenaded by hits from the Stones, the Who, Pink Floyd, Springsteen and stadium rock anthems from the '70s and '80s. Sticking to the beer is a good idea as it's very good value (bottle of Chang 49B); cocktails are pricier (100B). The walls are garlanded in posters from the golden age of rock, including a worthy shrine of Bowie album covers that has recently gone up in the far corner. (☏081 747 0937; Chaweng Beach Rd; ⏰3pm-2am)

Bar Ice
BAR

13 MAP P52, C2

For some a sub-zero novelty, Ice Bar – north of Chaweng Lake – is

entertaining, but it doesn't come cheap. Dress up in a padded coat and hat and sink a drink on the rocks in sub-zero temperatures surrounded by ice sculptures and visible breath. Children are welcome, too, and will love it – look for the family deals (per family 500B) on the website. (☏077 484933; Chaweng Lake Rd; ⏰5.30pm-2am)

Bees Knees Brewpub
BREWERY

14 MAP P52, B2

The rather charmless interior decor and downcast service win no prizes, but the beer (from 120B) – brewed on site – gets serious accolades and big thumbs-up. Choose from five beers (wheaty bee, summer bee, black bee, bitter bee or black-and-tan) and enjoy some deeply rich and thorough flavours. The brewery is right next to the bar, visible through glass. (☏085 537 2498; www.samuibrew.pub; Chaweng Lake Rd; ⏰3pm-1am)

Ark Bar BAR

15 MAP P52, D3

Drinks are dispensed from the multicoloured bar to an effusive crowd, guests recline on loungers on the beach, and the party is on day and night, with fire shows lighting up the sands after sundown and DJs providing house music from the afternoon onwards. (www.ark-bar.com; ⊙7am-1am)

Tropical Murphy's Irish BAR

16 MAP P52, C3

Come night-time, the live music kicks on and this place turns into the most popular Irish bar on Ko Samui (yes, there are quite a few), but it's a great place for a pint at any time. On the menu, there's steak-and-kidney pie, fish and chips, Ulster Fry (breakfast) and lamb chops and Irish stew (mains 60B to 300B). (📞077 413614; Chaweng Beach Rd; ⊙9am-1am; 📶)

Bar Solo BAR

17 MAP P52, D2

Bar Solo's neat lines, bubbly party mood, expert DJs and evening drink specials lure in front-loaders preparing for a late, late night at the dance clubs on Soi Solo and Soi Green Mango. (📞077 300466; Chaweng Beach Rd; ⊙6pm-1am)

Reggae Pub BAR

18 MAP P52, C3

This fortress of fun sports an open-air dance floor with music spun by foreign DJs. It's a towering

Ark Bar

Ko Samui's Beaches

Samui is just about small enough to beach-hop without too much difficulty and you'll encounter considerable variety along its sandy lengths. **Chaweng** is the longest strip, with many different moods, from its rocky and rather subdued north to a crowded and animated central area and the quieter **Chaweng Noi**. **Hat Lamai** sees the best swimming in the middle of its beach, but down in the south it's picturesquely studded with huge boulders.

Though seas are calmer from July to October, winds from the northeast rake the sands, causing swells from December to April, while riptides can make swimming in Chaweng and Lamai dangerous, even for strong swimmers.

Mae Nam has the best swimming beach on the north coast. On the west coast, the beaches at **Taling Ngam** and **Lipa Noi** are pleasant swimming choices. **Bo Phut** has rather coarse sand and the water is murkier, while in the northeast corner of the island, **Ao Thong Sai** is lovely. For a total escape, head down to **Ao Phang Ka** in the southwest.

two-storey affair with long bars, pool tables and a live-music stage. The whole place doubles as a shrine to Bob Marley; it's often empty early in the evening, getting going around midnight. The long road up to Reggae Pub is ladyboy central. (Laem Din Rd; 6pm-3am)

Entertainment

Paris Follies Cabaret

CABARET

19 MAP P52, D2

This dazzling and fun cabaret offers one-hour *gà·teu·i* (also spelled *kàthoey*) cabaret featuring cross-dresser and/or transgender performers every night at 8pm, 9pm, 10pm and 11pm and attracts a mixed clientele of both sexes. Admission is free, but you need to buy a drink (from around 300B). (Chaweng Beach Rd; 8pm-midnight)

Starz Cabaret

CABARET

20 MAP P52, D2

One of Chaweng's most popular and visible ladyboy cabaret shows, right at the pulsing heart of the district, with singers going through big hits. There's no entry fee, but you need to buy a compulsory first drink for at least 250B a pop (second drink half price). Shows are at 8.30pm, 9.30pm and 10.30pm. (Chaweng Beach Rd; 8pm-midnight)

Shopping

Central Festival
SHOPPING CENTRE

21 🔒 MAP P52, C3

This bright, shiny and huge monster-mall is stuffed with shops, cafes and restaurants and legions of Chinese shoppers. There's a terrific range of shopping options, and some of the dining choices are excellent too. There's a bouncy slide for kids. (Chaweng Beach Rd; ⏱11am-11pm)

Jim Thompson
CLOTHING

Elegant and attractive women's silk clothing, bags, dresses, blouses, scarves and much more, located in the Central Festival (see

21 🔒 Map p52, C3) mall. (📞077 410404; www.jim-thompson.com; Chaweng Beach Rd; ⏱11am-11pm)

Nature Art Gallery
JEWELLERY

22 🔒 MAP P52, C3

With a selection several notches above most of the tat for sale along Chaweng Beach Rd, this shop sells elegant, eye-catching and well-made jewellery, fashioned from gold, silver and precious stones. There's another branch on the 2nd floor of Central Festival mall. (📞077 422594, 081 370 1791; www.thailand-jewelry.com; Chaweng Beach Rd)

Central Festival shopping mall

SERGEY ZHUKOV/SHUTTERSTOCK ©

Explore ◉
Hat Lamai &
the Southeast

Lamai puts you within reach of some of the island's most famous waterfalls and wát, a choice of delightfully languorous beach views and some of Samui's best dining experiences. Don't overlook a trip south to the colourful coastal Muslim village of Ban Hua Thanon, a picture with its old fishing boats laying in the shallow waters beyond the lilting coconut palms.

Drop by Hat Lamai for the first flecks of early morning sun and catch the beach coming to life. Consider breakfast at Baobab (p73) or Black Pearl (p73) for supreme morning visuals in the early light. Later in the morning, steal a lead on the crowds to stop by the Na Muang Waterfalls (p64), before exploring all the Buddhist wát in the area; certainly don't miss Wat Racha Thammaram (p68) or Wat Samret (p68). If you've a scooter or bicycle, hop on our ride (see p78) from Ban Hua Thanon to Ao Phang Ka via the Laem Saw Pagoda (p69) and its fine views; otherwise, drop by Ban Hua Thanon (p71) in the afternoon and don't overlook visiting its beach for photogenic images of the moored boats. Tie up the day exploring Lamai's choice of restaurants and bars.

Getting There & Around

Hat Lamai is a major stop on the east coast and *sŏrng·tăa·ou* (pick-up minibuses) all drive through. Otherwise, it's a short, scenic and hilly drive on a scooter from Chaweng – make sure you stop off at the Lad Koh Viewpoint (p54) if you do the trip on a set of wheels.

Hat Lamai & the Southeast Map on p66

Top Experience
Na Muang Waterfalls

◎ MAP P66, A2

admission free

In the jungle interior in the south of the island, these two waterfalls are the most famous falls on Ko Samui. Note that most of the rain lands from November to December so things are in full flow through to February, and the waterfalls can run dry between March and June, but rainfall can vary so check with your accommodation before heading out.

Na Muang Waterfall

At 18m, this is the most famous waterfall on Samui and lies in the centre of the island about 7km west of Hat Lamai. During the rainy season, the water cascades over ethereal purple rocks, and there's a superb, large natural pool for swimming at the base (so pack your trunks), where the water is much cooler than at the beach (so be prepared). You can swim right up to the water crashing down on your head. This is the most scenic of Samui's falls, but prepare for limited action during the drier seasons. You can also walk down the river, or trek along a path into the trees in the area around the waterfall. Admission is free, but there's a small charge for parking your scooter.

Na Muang Waterfall 2

This waterfall falls a greater distance than at Na Muang Waterfall and admission is also free, but it's a slightly longer walk and unfortunately you need to go through the avoidable Na Muang Safari Park en route, though you can skip the 'attractions', which include feeling an elephant bananas, or having your photo taken with a leopard or a tiger – all for a fee, and not recommended. The safari park also encourages you to take one of its 100B rides up to the waterfall, but you can leg it, but bring decent shoes (especially if the way and rocks are slippery). The falls drop around 80m in all, and collect in another pool you can go for a dip in.

★ Top Tip

◦ Check on the water flow before you head out, take your swimming trunks and decent hiking shoes.

✕ Take a Break

There aren't many cafes or restaurants nearby, so pack some snacks and drinks with you and have a picnic on the rocks of the waterfalls.

Getting There

Scooter Head up to the falls off the 4169.

Taxi Around 500B from Lamai.

Hike Follow the signs off the 4169.

Tours Can be arranged through your hotel.

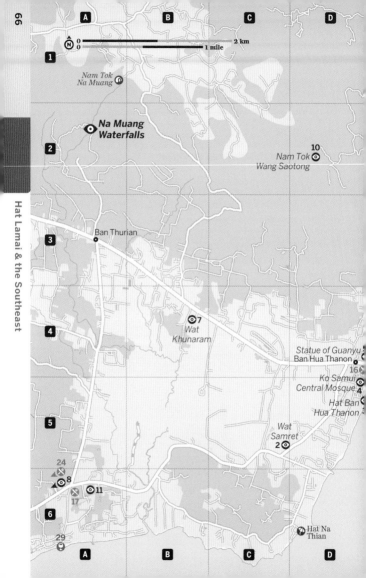

0
0

2 km
1 mile

Nam Tok
Na Muang

**Na Muang
Waterfalls**

10
Nam Tok
Wang Saotong

Ban Thurian

7
Wat
Khunaram

Statue of Guanyu
Ban Hua Thanon

16
Ko Samui
Central Mosque 4

Hat Ban
Hua Thanon

Wat
Samret
2

24
8
17 11

29

Hat Na
Thian

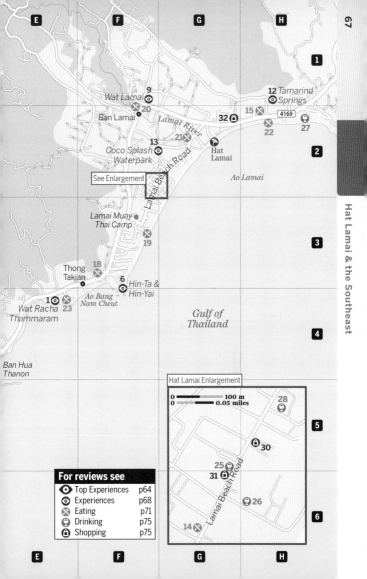

Hat Lamai & the Southeast

E   F   G   H

1

Wat Lamai
9
20
Ban Lamai
Lamai River
12 *Tamarind Springs*
15
32
4169
22
27

2

13
Coco Splash
Waterpark
21
Lamai Beach Road
Hat
Lamai
Ao Lamai

See Enlargement

Lamai Muay
Thai Camp
19

3

Thong
Takian
18
6 Hin-Ta &
Hin-Yai
*Ao Bang
Nam Cheut*
*Gulf of
Thailand*

1
23
Wat Racha
Thammaram

4

*Ban Hua
Thanon*

Hat Lamai Enlargement

0   100 m
0   0.05 miles
28

5

30

25
31
Lamai Beach Road
26

14

6

For reviews see

◉	Top Experiences	p64
◉	Experiences	p68
✕	Eating	p71
⊕	Drinking	p75
🔒	Shopping	p75

E   F   G   H

Experiences

Wat Racha Thammaram
BUDDHIST TEMPLE

1 ⊙ MAP P66, E4

This temple (the name means Snake Stone Temple) on the south side of Rte 4169 has a recently built red-clay temple hall, decorated with a fascinating display of bas-relief designs and statues. It's an astonishing sight against the blue sky. A golden pagoda contains relics of Sakyamuni, and a sacred bodhi tree also grows within the grounds. From the pagoda, steps head down to a collection of stupas, commemorating former monks. (Wat Sila Ngu; off Rte 4169; admission free; ◷dawn–dusk)

Wat Samret
BUDDHIST TEMPLE

2 ⊙ MAP P66, C5

At Wat Samret, near Th Ban Hua, you can see a typical Mandalay sitting Buddha carved from solid marble – a common sight in India and northern Thailand, but not so common in the south. There is also a long reclining buddha (representing Sakyamuni about to enter parinirvana) with a very peaceful countenance in another hall, surrounded by a galaxy of other Buddhist figures; at the rear of the temple ground is a forest of mouldering stupas. (Maret Temple; off Rte 4170; admission free; ◷dawn–dusk)

Hat Ban Hua Thanon
BEACH

3 ⊙ MAP P66, D5

There might be quite a lot of rubbish here, but this beach just south of the Muslim village of Ban Hua Thanon (p71) is a picture for its fishing vessels moored in the water, ancient, disintegrating boats on the sand, kids playing around and the palm tree forest that comes right up to the sand. It's a very photogenic area, and doesn't attract sunloungers or sunseekers, just those keen to discover weather-beaten texture and charming vistas.

Ko Samui Central Mosque
MOSQUE

4 ⊙ MAP P66, D5

At the heart of the community, this delightful green, gold and white painted mosque is in Ban Hua Thanon, along the main drag as you head towards the beach.

Statue of Guanyu
STATUE

5 ⊙ MAP P66, D4

A sign of the mushrooming Chinese tourism to the island, and of Chinese patronage, is this recently constructed colossal statue of Guanyu (also called Guandi). Guanyu was a 3rd-century general from the Three Kingdoms period who is also worshipped as a deity representing martial valour and is often referred to as the God of War. There is also a temple here, colourfully garlanded with banners and a host of smaller statues, including one of Guanyin. (Ban Hua Thanon)

Hin-Ta & Hin-Yai   LANDMARK

6 ◎ MAP P66, F3

At the south end of Hat Lamai, you'll find these infamous genitalia-shaped stone formations (also known as Grandfather and Grandmother Rocks) that provide endless mirth for giggling Thai tourists.

Wat Khunaram   BUDDHIST TEMPLE

7 ◎ MAP P66, B4

South of Rte 4169 between Th Ban Thurian and Th Ban Hua, Wat Khunaram contains the mummi-

fied remains of a pious monk. The temple abbot, Luang Phaw Daeng, has been dead for over four decades but his corpse is preserved sitting in a meditative pose and sporting a pair of sunglasses. The monk foresaw his own death in 1973, when he had reached the age of 79. (off Rte 4169; admission free; ⏱dawn-dusk)

Laem Saw Pagoda   BUDDHIST TEMPLE

8 ◎ MAP P66, A6

Framed against the sea, Laem Saw Pagoda, at the southern end of Samui, is home to an intriguing, highly venerated old Srivijaya-style stupa with scenic views over the water. (Lam Sho Rd; admission free; ⏱dawn-dusk)

Hat Ban Hua Thanon

Wat Lamai

BUDDHIST TEMPLE

9 MAP P66, F1

Right at the sharp bend in the road along Rte 4169, this simple temple is worth an exploration as a diversion from Lamai beach life. There's a folklore museum containing a display of Buddhist artefacts and relics associated with the history of Ko Samui. (admission free; ☼dawn-dusk)

Nam Tok Wang Saotong

WATERFALL

10 ◎ MAP P66, D2

This high-drop waterfall is just north of the ring road near Ban Hua Thanon. There are signs warning visitors not to climb the falls as there have been fatalities.

Koh Samui Rum

DISTILLERY

11 ◎ MAP P66, A6

The only rum distillery in Thailand produces Caribbean agricole-style spirits (distilled from fresh, fermented sugarcane juice) in a variety of all natural flavours, including a delectable coconut rum obtained from soaking co-conut meat in the rum for several months. There's a video about the production process, a tasting area, an excellent French-Thai restaurant and a shop in beautiful palm-shaded surrounds. (📱091 816 7416; www.rum-distillery.com; Ban Bang Kao; tasting shots 50-75B; ☼9am-6pm)

Tamarind Springs

Tamarind Springs

MASSAGE

12 MAP P66, H1

Tucked far away from the beach within a silent coconut-palm plantation, Tamarind's small collection of villas and massage studios is seamlessly incorporated into nature: some have granite boulders built into walls and floors, while others offer private ponds or creative outdoor baths. There's also a superhealthy restaurant and packages for three-night or longer stays in the elegant villas and suites. (📞 080 569 6654; www.tamarindsprings.com; off Rte 4169; spa packages from 1500B)

Coco Splash Waterpark

WATER PARK

13 MAP P66, F2

Kids under 10 will love this small park of painted concrete water slides. Towel hire is 60B (200B deposit) and there's a restaurant (open till 10pm). Note that if you're planning on watching the kids and not going in the water yourself, you get in for free. Those under 1.5m get a T-shirt thrown in; if you're over 1.5m, it's a cocktail. (📞 081 082 6035; www.samuiwaterpark.com; Ban Lamai; over/under 1.5m 349/329B, under 0.9m free; ⏱10.30am-5.30pm)

Visiting Ban Hua Thanon

Just south of Hat Lamai, **Ban Hua Thanon** (Map p66, E4) is full of photo-ops and home to a vibrant Muslim community; its anchorage of high-bowed fishing vessels by the almost deserted beach (p68) through the palm trees at the end of the community is a veritable gallery of intricate designs, though it's a shame about all the rubbish on the sand. Look out for the green, gold and white mosque (p68) in the village, along the main drag and near the bustling market (p72).

Eating

Kangaroo

THAI $

14 MAP P66, G6

Colourful, efficient and friendly Kangaroo serves excellent Thai and Western dishes, and a wealth of succulent seafood, including shark steak, barracuda steak and blue crab as well as more standard chicken curries, sizzling platters, fried-rice dishes and pasta. (Lamai Beach Rd; mains from 120B; ⏱1-11pm)

On the Beach at Buffalo Baby

Way down on the south shore at Ao Bang Kao, fun beachside bar **Buffalo Baby** (Map p66, A6; Bang Kao), run by the affable Maurice, really comes alive on Saturdays at 5pm when the Bang Kao Walking Street, a buzzing market set to live music on a stage right on the sand, takes off. Occasional fire shows lighting up the sands are also on the menu, while the bar also has a DJ on Saturdays. The walking street is a work in progress and growing all the time, so check ahead to see what's cookin'.

Pad Thai

THAI $

15 MAP P66, H2

On the corner of the huge Manathai hotel by the road, this highly affordable, semi-alfresco and smart restaurant is a fantastic choice for stir-fried and soup noodles, rounded off with a coconut ice cream. (☎077 458560-4; www.manathai.com/samui/phad-thai; Rte 4169; mains from 70B; ⏰11am-9.30pm)

Hua Thanon Market

MARKET $

16 MAP P66, D4

Slip into the rhythm of this village market slightly south of Lamai; it's a window into the food ways of southern Thailand. Vendors shoo away the flies from the freshly butchered meat, and housewives load bundles of vegetables into their baby-filled motorcycle baskets. Follow the market road to the row of food shops delivering edible Muslim culture: chicken biryani, fiery curries or toasted rice with coconut, bean sprouts, lemon grass and dried shrimp. (Ban Hua Thanon; dishes from 30B; ⏰6am-6pm)

Sweet Sisters Cafe

CAFE $

17 MAP P66, A6

Charming, cosy and with an enticing interior, this roadside cafe down in the quiet south of Ko Samui, just before the turn-off for Ao Bang Kao, is a welcoming place for shots of caffeine, juices and snacks as you explore the beaches, bays and pagodas of the southern shore. (Bang Kao; ⏰11am-9pm;)

Lamai Day Market

MARKET $

18 MAP P66, F3

Lamai's market is a hive of activity, selling food necessities and takeaway food. Visit the covered area to pick up fresh fruit or to see vendors shredding coconuts to make coconut milk. Or hunt down the ice-cream seller for homemade coconut ice cream. It's next door to a petrol station. (Lamai; dishes from 30B; ⏱6am-8pm)

Baobab
FRENCH $$

19 ✕ MAP P66, F3

Grab a free beach towel and crash out on a sun lounger after a full meal at breezy Baobab, or have a massage next door, but seize one of the beach tables (if you can). You'll need two hands to turn over the hefty menu, with its all-day breakfasts, French/Thai dishes, grills, pastas and popular specials, including red tuna steak.

With the sound of the surf and lovely views it's frequently a sell-out. (☎084 838 3040; Hat Lamai; mains 150-380B; ⏱8am-6pm)

La Fabrique
BAKERY $$

20 ✕ MAP P66, F2

Ceiling fans chop the air and service is snappy and helpful at this roomy French-style boulangerie/patisserie away from the main drag, near Wat Lamai on Rte 4169. *The* place for brekkie, select from fresh bread, croissants, gratins, baguettes, meringues, yoghurts, pastries or unusually good set breakfasts that include fresh fruit. Wash down with a decent selection of coffees or teas. (☎077 961507; Rte 4169; set breakfasts from 120B; ⏱6.30am-10.30pm; 🛜)

Black Pearl
THAI $$

This decent restaurant has a gorgeous perspective on the sea,

Lamai Walking Street Night Market (p75)

Ko Taen & Ko Mat Sum

For sensations of the small castaway islands offshore from Ko Samui and to flee the crowded east coast, head south and bounce over the waves on a long-tail fishing boat to Ko Taen (also spelled Ko Tan) and Ko Mat Sum, two sparsely populated islands accessible from the village and bay of Thong Krut on the southwest shore.

The larger of the two islands at 7.5 sq km, Ko Taen has some very good snorkelling and a couple of guesthouses, including Koh Tan Village Bungalows on the main beach, as well as several restaurants.

Ko Mat Sum is a much smaller and far less inhabited island a kilometre or so east of Ko Taen, with a simple guesthouse and a bar.

You'll see signs in Thong Krut advertising boats, or pop into one of the guesthouses or beachfront restaurants – such as **Hemingway's on the Beach** (Map p66, A6; ☏ 088 452 4433; off Rte 4170, Ao Thong Krut; mains from 175B; ⏱10am-8pm Sat, Mon, Tue & Thu, 10am-6pm Sun) – and ask. Trips usually last four to five hours and cost from 2000B to 2500B for the boat (seating up to five people) and may include a drink.

from a beautiful stretch of Lamai sand peppered with boulders (see 19 ⊗ Map p66, F3). It's lovely throughout the day, but twilight, with a cocktail and the lapping of the surf, is a very pleasant time to arrive. (Mains 140-450B; ⏱8am-10.30pm; 🛜)

Tandoori Nights INDIAN $$

21 ⊗ MAP P66, G2

The set meals at this welcoming Indian restaurant will only set you back 190B for a vegetable curry, soft drink and a papadum; otherwise select your spice level from the à la carte menu or take a deep breath and order the eye-watering lamb vindaloo, quenched with a chilled beer. (☏091 161 7026; Lamai; mains from 150B; ⏱11am-11pm)

Radiance INTERNATIONAL $$

22 ⊗ MAP P66, H2

Healthy food rarely tastes this good. It's not all brown rice or full of vegans: you'll find everything from an amazing raw *thom kha* (coconut green curry soup) to chocolate smoothies that can jive with anyone's dietary restrictions. Plus the semi-outdoor beach-side setting is tranquil, relaxing and unpretentious. (off Rte 4169; meals 100-400B; ⏱7am-10pm; 🛜🖊🖉)

The Dining Room FRENCH $$$

23 ⊗ MAP P66, E4

The signature beef Rossini at this fantastically positioned beachfront restaurant at **Rocky's Resort** (📞077 418367; www.rockyresort. com; off Rte 4169; r 8000-20,000B; ❄🛜♨) is like sending your taste buds on a Parisian vacation as the views pop you into seventh heaven. (dishes 300-950B; 🕐lunch & dinner)

Drinking

Samui Shamrock Irish Pub
PUB

25 🚇 MAP P66, G5

With live music every night from 9.30pm and a decent enough Western and Thai menu (including breakfasts), the Shamrock has a range of fine Irish whiskies, Guinness and Kilkenny on tap, with Tiger for more pedestrian tastes. Staff are friendly, the food is good value and the rollicking atmosphere when the live band kicks off is fun. (www.thesamuishamrock. com; Lamai Beach Rd; mains from 70B; 🕐9.30am-1am)

Lava Lounge
BAR

26 🚇 MAP P66, H6

One of the better bars in Hat Lamai, Lava Lounge is a chilled-out spot with an invigorating menu of cocktails (99B to 150B), and a happy hour that runs from 4pm to 9pm, which includes a spirit with mixer for 79B. (📞080 886 5035; Hat Lamai; 🕐4pm-2am)

Beach Republic
BAR

27 🚇 MAP P66, H2

Recognised by its yawning thatch-patched awnings, Beach Republic could be the poster child of a made-for-TV, beachside, booze-swilling holiday. There's a wading pool, comfy lounge chairs, an endless cocktail list and even a hotel if you never, ever want to leave the party. The Sunday brunches (11.30am to 3.30pm) here are legendary. (📞077 458100; www. beachrepublic.com; 176/34 Mu 4, Hat Lamai; 🕐7am-11pm)

Bear Cocktails
BAR

28 🚇 MAP P66, H5

It's not a traditional bar, but a fun, open-air cocktail stall on the road run by some friendly girls (Bear and Lek); buy a strawberry daiquiri, grab a plastic seat and chat to whoever's at hand. It's not far from the McDonald's; cocktails are 79B. (Lamai Beach Rd; 🕐5pm-2am)

Shopping

Lamai Walking Street Night Market
MARKET

30 🔒 MAP P66, H5

Lamai's night market kicks off on Sundays – it's an excellent and fun time to browse for bargains and hunt for street food. Keep an eye on your bag as pickpockets are prevalent. (🕐4-10pm Sun)

Island Books

BOOKS

31 🔒 MAP P66, G6

With a wealth of titles, this smaller branch of Island books is located at the heart of Lamai. (📞 061 193 2132; www.island-books-samui.com; 🕐 9am-7pm)

Island Books

BOOKS

32 🔒 MAP P66, G2

Tucked away on a lane off the 4169 and run by Liverpudlian Paul, this larger branch of Island Books is on the main drag past Lamai. It has the largest selection of used books – in pretty much every language – on the island. (off Rte 4169; 🕐 9am-7pm)

Muay Thai competitors perform the ritual dance

Understanding Muay Thai

Also known as Thai boxing, *muay Thai* (also spelt *moo·ay tai*) is a blistering, explosive and highly dynamic fighting art involving punches, kicks and strikes, as well as clinches. Known as the 'Art of Eight Limbs', the combat sport aims to employ the entire body as a weapon, with a focus on the hands, elbows, knees and feet.

Punches, Kicks & Endurance

Punches include jabs, straight punches, hooks, uppercuts and swings, while the most common kicks are the front jab, the hook kick, the diagonal kick and the roundhouse, often delivered to the opponent's leg or knee with the shin to cause debilitating pain. As *muay Thai* fighters heavily use the bone for strikes, they extensively condition their rock-hard shin bones.

Thai boxers are also known for the endurance training, practising moves for up to six hours a day. Unlike many other Asian martial arts such as Wing Chun, Taekwondo or Karate-do, Thai boxers focus their training around real fights rather than performing patterns or forms. This focus, coupled with the intense conditioning, high levels of fitness and seasoned fighting experience makes Thai boxers particularly tough opponents, although careers are short for professionals, as fighters burn out quickly.

Ritual Dance

Before a competition match starts, fighters wear a *Mongkol* headband as well as *Pra Jiad* (armbands) and perform the *Wai khru ram muay* ritual dance that precedes fights, with the fighter circling the ring in a counter-clockwise direction and then praying, bowing the head three times, while music is played. The ritual is performed to show respect to the fighter's coach and school.

Muay Thai Schools

Schools and gyms on Ko Samui, Ko Pha-Ngan and Ko Tao can offer introductory classes, full courses or refresher courses for experienced fighters and many also provide accommodation. The oldest and most established Thai boxing club on the island is the **Lamai Muay Thai Camp** (Map p66, F3; ☏087 082 6970; www.lamaimuaythai camp.com; 82/2 Mu 3, Lamai; day/week training sessions 300/1500B; ⊙7am-8pm). There are also several places you can watch competition fights in Chaweng – you can't miss the vans advertising bouts every night along Chaweng Beach Rd.

Cycling Tour 🚲

The South Coast's Villages & Temples

Cycle through this area of coconut plantations, past sacred temples, Buddhist effigies, small communities and narrow roads through tall palms, a pagoda, a rum distillery and beautiful bays, before coming to rest in the far west of the island at Ao Phang Ka, one of the quietest stretches of sand on Ko Samui.

Route Facts

Start Ban Hua Thanon
End Ao Phang Ka
Length 15km; 3 hours

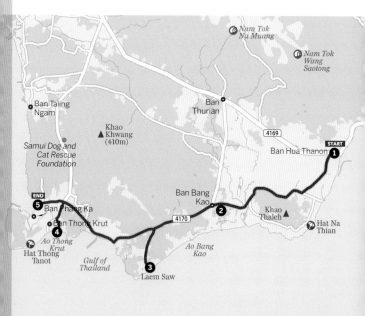

❶ Ban Hua Thanon

Head off the 4169 to explore the Muslim village of Ban Hua Thanon (p71), where you can walk down the main market street, admiring the mosque and exploring the beach through the palm trees beyond, to the traditional boats lying in shallow water. The huge statue to the north of the village is of Guanyu, a Chinese hero and deity (p68).

❷ Koh Samui Rum

Head out along the 4169 and then turn left down the 4170, passing a sign for Ban Thong Krut (8km). For a short diversion from here, you will see a sign for Wat Samret to your right along Thanon Proo-Na-Muang, otherwise continue in the same direction to the Koh Samui Rum distillery (p70), which is well worth exploring. If you want a coffee, stop off at the nearby Sweet Sisters Cafe (p72), near the corner of Th Ban Kao.

❸ Laem Saw Pagoda

At the Sweet Sisters Cafe junction, you can turn right and cycle up the 4173 for a short distance and find a golden seated Buddha effigy beneath a pavilion on the left-hand side of the road. Backtracking and continuing along the 4170, look out for Lam Sho Road, which turns off to the left and leads down to the sea. At the end of the road stands the Laem Saw Pagoda (p69), with superb views out across the water.

❹ Ao Thong Krut

Keep cycling along the 4170 till it runs into the community around Ao Thong Krut on the bay. Walk along the beach, or stop in Hemingway's on the Beach (p74), an excellent choice for lunch or a drink. Look out for signs for long-tail boats making the trip to the islands of Ko Taen and Ko Mat Sum (p74).

❺ Ao Phang Ka

Continue along the 4170 and cross the crossroads with Thanon Keeree Mas (Keeree Mas Road) and go straight on, without turning left or right. The road will bring you to the lovely bay of Ao Phang Ka, which will – if you time your journey for the late afternoon – reward you with a delightful sunset. Out on the sands, you'll feel a million miles from frantic Chaweng.

Mae Nam &
the North Coast

Mae Nam's slim length of white sand slopes down to a calm and swimmable aqua sea. One of the island's prettiest stretches of beach, it's popular with families and older couples, giving it an unhurried yet vibrant ambience – perfect for reading in the shade of a coconut tree or indulging in beach massages. The town is a charmer too, with all the rhythms of Thai life, from bustling school children, to busy locals shopping in the market and restaurateurs throwing open the doors of their eateries.

Early morning on Mae Nam beach is an ideal time to arrive in the neighbourhood and pay a visit to the colourful Mae Nam Chinese Temple (p83). Later, consider heading uphill into the jungle to the Mae Nam Viewpoint (p83) as well as the Tan Rua Waterfall (p85) and above that, the View Top (p85), for superb views from the spine of the island. Consider walking along the shoreline to the Buddhist statue around the headland. Sunset from Beryl Bar (p88) is another highlight, but a twilight wander along the sands of either Mae Nam Beach or Bo Phut Beach is an atmospheric and romantic conclusion to the day too. Further romance can be found dining at Farmer (p87) or John's Garden Restaurant (p87).

Getting There & Around

Located west of Bo Phut, Mae Nam is easily reached by scooter, round-island *sǒrng·tǎa·ou* (pick-up mini-bus), taxi or on foot.

Mae Nam & the North Coast Map on p84

Mae Nam Beach (p83) PARASOLA PARASOLA/GETTY IMAGES ©

Top Experience
Around Mae Nam

The main draw is Mae Nam beach, a largely unhurried 5km length of sand, perfect for relaxation and dipping into a chunky novel to the sound of the waves. Once you've tired of lying on the beach, Mae Nam is also the starting point of a terrific scooter journey, or hike, to the Mae Nam Viewpoint and an even higher perspective over the island from the View Top.

◉ MAP P84, E1

Twilight Walk along the Beach

Fringed with swaying coconut trees, Mae Nam Beach (p82) is the best beach on the north coast, with relatively low visitor numbers and far fewer vendors than hopping Chaweng Beach. After a day of sunbathing and swimming, set off on a long walk east as the sun begins to dip to catch it at its most romantic with the sea turning silver. Early morning is also a good time.

Mae Nam Chinese Temple

Just a few steps from the sand and under the dazzling Ko Samui sun and an azure sky, this vibrantly coloured **Chinese temple** (Map p84, E1; pictured) is a blaze of red, blue, green, gold, yellow and decorative murals from Chinese myth and legend coating its walls. Dragons writhe in all directions while a small Chinese pavilion stands closer to the sea looking over the beach and out onto the blue waves. The Chinese New Year sees the temple at its brightest best.

Mae Nam Walking Street

Mae Nam's bustling **walking street** (Map p84, E2; ⏱ from 5pm Thu) kicks off on Thursday evenings, through China Town, a long street fronted by a Chinese gateway. At all other times, it's a popular choice for cheap post-beach cocktails (from mobile vendors) and heaps of street food, as well as clothes, souvenirs and knick-knacks. If you want to graze, snack or eat a full-on lunch or dinner, head here for oodles of choice.

Mae Nam Viewpoint

Jump on a scooter to whisk yourself to the **Mae Nam Viewpoint** (Map p84, E4; 50B), which looks down onto the canopy below and a gorgeous, endless view unfolds beneath you to the sea. The Tan Rua Waterfall is a short walk away, or you can carry on up to the View Top even higher up and with even more mesmerising panoramas across the treetops and the gulf.

★ **Top Tips**

○ Consider packing a picnic for lunch on the beach.

○ Watch out for glass in the sand; if walking along the beach at dusk, wear sandals.

🍴 **Take a Break**

Lap up some excellent Korean food at the Gaon Korean Restaurant (p86), right at the heart of things or for delightful Pan-Asian cuisine, Fish Restaurant (p86) is also central and easy to reach.

Mae Nam & the North Coast

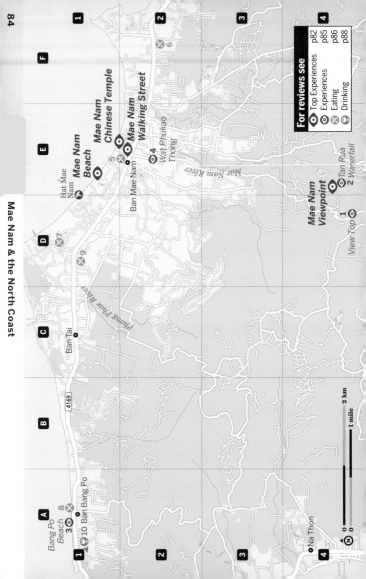

Bang Po Beach
Ban Bang Po
Ban Tai
Phang Phae River
4169
Na Thon

Mae Nam Beach
Hat Mae Nam
Mae Nam Chinese Temple
Mae Nam Walking Street
Ban Mae Nam
Mae Nam River
Wat Phukao Thong

Mae Nam Viewpoint
Tan Rua Waterfall
View Top

2 km
1 mile

Experiences

View Top
VIEWPOINT

1 ⊙ MAP P84, D4

For the best views over the island, take your scooter up to the View Top past the Mae Nam Viewpoint. There are some pretty steep switchbacks on the way up near the top, but you'll be rewarded with some stunning views, over the jungle interior and out to sea and Ko Pha-Ngan. A small line of bungalow-style cabins serves drinks and a sign advises scooter drivers to periodically stop to let their brakes cool on the way down.

Keep walking or driving a bit past the cabins to a large rock on the left, where you can stand for astonishing views.

Tan Rua Waterfall
WATERFALL

2 ⊙ MAP P84, E4

A short walk up the dilapidated wooden steps and along the path through the trees from the Mae Nam Viewpoint (p83) brings you to this lovely waterfall, which spills down through tendrils of green foliage high up in the hills. Backtracking a bit is another section of waterfall before you reach the main falls, which guide you down to another section of falls where you can clamber over the rocks – hold on tight to the rope as it's slippery.

Bang Po Beach
BEACH

3 ⊙ MAP P84, A1

Stretching over several kilometres, this beach along the northern

Bang Po Beach

JARNATYONGYSHUTTERSTOCK ©

shore towards the northeast tip of the island is a quiet length of sand; it's an excellent choice for escaping the crowds. (Bang Po)

Wat Phukao Thong
BUDDHIST TEMPLE

4 ◉ MAP P84, E2

A dark Buddha is seated under a golden pavilion up a long flight of steps lined with glittering green dragon banisters at this quiet wát up from the main road. There's also a handsome main hall decorated in red, gold and green. (Mae Nam)

Eating

Fish Restaurant
INTERNATIONAL $

5 ✕ MAP P84, E2

With elegant Thai tablecloths and a well-priced, tasty menu of Thai seafood and pan-Asian dishes and international appetisers, this popular wood-floored eatery pulls in a regular stream of diners for its charming setting, winning spring rolls, gorgeous seafood curries, steamed sea bass and much more. (☏ 087 472 4097; Rte 4169, Mae Nam; mains from 50B; ⏰ 11am-11pm)

Pepenero
ITALIAN $$

6 ✕ MAP P84, F2

Pepenero continues to cause a stir on Ko Samui, moving to this more accessible Mae Nam location. What this excellent and neatly designed Italian restaurant lacks in views is more than made up for by a terrific menu (including cutting boards with cheese and cold cuts) and the care and attention displayed to customers by the very sociable, hard-working hosts. Put this one in your planner.

No credit cards, but you can settle in a variety of currencies or with PayPal. (☏ 077 963353; www.pepenerosamui.com; Mae Nam; mains from 250B; ⏰ 6-10pm Mon-Sat)

Gaon Korean Restaurant
KOREAN $$

Right in China Town in Mae Nam (see 5 ✕ Map p84, E2), this excellent restaurant offers barbecued meat, grilled fish and steamed seafood sets, as well as Korean staples such as delicious *bulgogi* (marinated beef with mushroom and carrot on a hot plate), kimchi pancake, Korean ice cream, a kids' menu and a range of sizzling choices for vegetarians. (mains from 180B; ⏰ 3-11pm)

Chinese New Year

The temple is a bundle of colour anyway, but if you're on Ko Samui during the Chinese New Year, head to the Mae Nam Chinese Temple (p83) to witness colourful Spring Festival parades, lion dances and spring festival festivities and to catch the temple at its vibrant best.

Chinese Temples

Attracting Thai-Chinese worshippers, or just those culturally interested in their Chinese roots, most Chinese temples on Ko Samui and Ko Pha-Ngan are very colourful buildings.

They differ in many ways from the Thai *wát*: they are usually much smaller and are frequently not Buddhist, or are multi-faith. Mae Nam Chinese Temple (p83) is not Buddhist, but is instead a shrine dedicated to folk religion and religious (not philosophical) Taoist belief, which is typical of the southern Chinese provinces from where most Thai-Chinese can trace their roots. The Hainan Temple (p98) in Na Thon is more akin to a guildhall than a temple, so is more a place where a clan would worship.

Chinese temples on Ko Samui generally obey Chinese rules of temple layout, with a clear sequence of halls on a line plus a single enveloping exterior wall, within which temple halls and courtyards muster. Chinese temples on Ko Samui are far smaller and younger than most temples in China and their use of colour is more vibrant than their more sober, yet grander, Chinese cousins.

John's Garden Restaurant
THAI $$

 7   MAP P84, D1

This delightful garden restaurant is a picture, with tables slung out beneath bamboo and palms and carefully cropped hedges. It's particularly romantic when lantern-lit at night, so reserve ahead, but pack some mosquito repellent (which is generally provided, but it's good to have backup).

The signature dish on the Thai and European menu is the excellent massaman chicken. (077 247694; www.johnsgarden samui.com; Mae Nam; mains from 160B; 1-10pm)

Bang Po Seafood
SEAFOOD $$

8   MAP P84, A1

A meal at Bang Po Seafood is a test for the taste buds. It's one of the only restaurants that serves traditional Ko Samui fare: recipes call for ingredients such as raw sea urchin roe, baby octopus, sea water, coconut and local turmeric. (Bang Po; dishes from 100B; dinner)

Farmer
INTERNATIONAL $$$

9   MAP P84, D1

Magically set in front of a photogenic rice field with green hills in the distance, fantastic Farmer –

Shoreline Hop

An undemanding but intriguing hike runs from Beryl Bar, near the northwest tip of the island, north along the rocky shoreline to a Buddhist statue that sits gazing out to sea. The hike is only a few hundred metres, so it's a very easy journey, though you'll be picking your way over the rocks. As you meander along the shoreline, note the fossilised coral and brooding dark geology of the coast. After around 10 minutes, you may notice a golden figure or two peeking out from the rock face; upon rounding a cliff, you'll see a large figure seated just around the corner.

within the boutique resort of the same name – is a choice selection, especially when the candlelight flickers on a starry night. The mostly European-inspired food is lovely and well-presented, there's a free pick-up for nearby beaches, and service is attentive.

Look out for the affordable set lunches; set breakfasts are 490B. Last orders are at 9.30pm. (☏077 447222; www.farmersboutiqueresort. com/restaurant; Mae Nam; mains 300-1500B, set lunch 250-340B; ☺7am-10.30pm)

Drinking

Beryl Bar   BAR

10 MAP P84, A1

The rather beaten up Beryl Bar has a colossal, slowly dilapidating and surreal statue of Santa Claus, and no wi-fi, but the remoteness and sense of tranquillity is the appeal here, with an end-of-the-world feel. Head north around the shore to discover a temple cave, with a seated statue outside, in a meditative posture. Sunsets from here are naturally divine.

The Thai menu is particularly good, so worth considering for dinner (or lunch), too. (Hat Laem Yai)

Coastal & Marine Degradation

Thailand's coastal regions have experienced higher population and economic growth than the national average, increasing pressure on the environment.

Soil Erosion & Water Quality

Soil erosion is a major coastal problem: it is estimated by the Department of Mineral Resources that approximately 5m of coastline per year is lost. This is due to coastal development (construction of jetties, breakwaters, oceanfront hotels and roads), land subsiding (due to groundwater depletion) and rising sea levels. Accurate data is lacking on coastal water quality, but analysts admit that wastewater treatment facilities are outpaced by the area's population and that industrial wastewater is often insufficiently treated. Coastal degradation puts serious pressure on Thailand's diverse coral reef system and marine environment.

Rising Sea Temperatures

Another risk factor is rising sea temperatures associated with El Niño weather conditions. High water temperatures cause coral bleaching and coral death. More than 10 dive sites in Thailand were closed in 2016 due to bleaching. Between 40% and 80% of the reefs on the Gulf and Andaman coasts were affected. A similar El Niño–related event occurred in 2010. Eighteen areas in seven marine parks that had experienced widespread bleaching were closed to tourism. Many of the reefs, especially in shallow water, never recovered. It is estimated that about 50% of Thailand's coral reefs are classified as highly threatened, indicating a disproportionate number of dead coral to living coral, according to a World Bank 2006 environmental report.

Over-Fishing

The overall health of the ocean is further impacted by large-scale fishing. Fisheries continue to experience declining catches as fish stocks plummet, and the industry is now dominated by big commercial enterprises that can go into deeper waters, focus more resources on a profitable catch and are less troubled by fines imposed on vessels that flout laws designed to protect fish stocks.

Walking Tour

Mae Nam
Viewpoint Trek

Take a journey from sea level up to a terrific viewpoint with ranging views over the island, via a waterfall deep in the jungle. The journey is doable on foot, but will take several hours to the waterfall and first view point and a further hour or so to the highest view point; by scooter it's far quicker. If you do walk, pack lots of water and wear decent shoes. The journey roughly follows the length of the Mae Nam River.

Walk Facts

Start Mae Nam

End View Top

Length 5.5km; 30 minutes driving or two hours walking

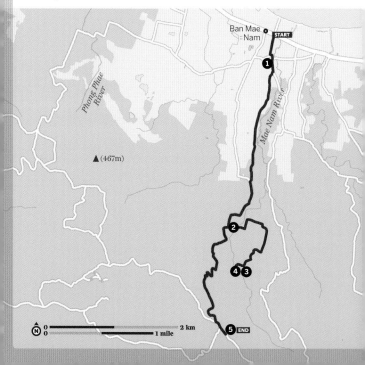

❶ Wat Phukao Thong

Ride your scooter south along Soi 4 from the Chinatown archway to this quiet temple on the corner and enter to explore and climb the green dragon lined steps. Follow the road as it hugs the temple to the left and go straight before taking the first right soon after the stupas at the rear of the temple and follow the waterfall sign.

❷ Tarzan Restaurant

Keep going for around 3km kilometres then turn left again to waterfall sign and continue till you see sign for Tarzan and Canopy Adventures/Secret Waterfall. Up ahead on your right is a Tarzan Restaurant, where you can stop for a coffee and a bite to eat.

❸ Canopy Adventures, Secret Falls & Viewpoint

As the road immediately beyond Tarzan Restaurant is impass-able on wheels, back track to the turning, head right and continue along the reddish, sandy road (it's pitted and craggy, so go carefully, or leave your scooter at Tarzan if it's wet) for around 1km to **Canopy Adventures** (☎077 300340; www.canopyadventuresthailand.com), where you can either try the zipline (2950B), or walk across (50B) to a wooden platform and viewpoint.

❹ Tan Rua Waterfall

Walk another 10 minutes from Canopy Adventures over some rather dilapidated wooden steps to where the Tan Rua waterfall (p85) – you can clamber over the rocks and admire the water as it spills through green vegetation – gushes over rocks and into a pool.

❺ View Top

Backtrack to Tarzan and turn left at the fork in the road and then left again up the switchbacks to the View Top (p85) for superb views. It's possible to continue to Na Thon, but the road is not good. If scootering back to Mae Nam, rest your brakes regularly down the switchbacks – it's a steep gradient.

❌ Take a Break

Grab a coffee and head out to the Viewpoint platform at the Canopy Adventures Cafe; there's wi-fi here, but you'll likely be too busy admiring the superb views. It does snacks too, including fried noodles or mango salad.

Explore ✦
Na Thon & the West

Samui's west coast is a welcome escape from the east-side bustle and is a quieter and slower-paced shopping alternative to Chaweng. It has skinny beaches of grainy sand, but the sunsets can be breathtaking, and the blue seas and views are beguiling. Na Thon is the main hub, where the boats pull in, while some of the island's best resorts cling to the coastline further south.

Explore Na Thon early in the morning when it's less busy and the town is coming to life. Admire the Hainan Temple (p98), in all its splendid colour before hiking up to the waterfall of Nam Tok Hin Lat (p96) and returning via the modest Coconut Museum (p97). For lunch head up into the hills again to the Phootawan Restaurant (p98) before moving down the coast in the afternoon to the secluded and tranquil bay at Ao Phang Ka. Sunsets are what the west coast is all about, so line up a meal at one of the seaside restaurants – try Five Islands (p98), Big John's Seafood Restaurant (p98) or Lucky (p98). Stop for stunning views over the gulf and fabulous cocktails at Air Bar (p99), before concluding your day with a walk along the beach at Na Thon.

Getting There & Around

Na Thon is connected by ferry to Don Sak (for Surat Thani) on the mainland, and the island of Ko Pha-Ngan and Ko Tao. The town is linked to other settlements around Ko Samui by *sŏrng·tăa·ou* (pick-up minibus), taxi, scooter, motorbike or bicycle.

Na Thon & the West Map on p94

Fishing boat off Na Thon Beach (p96) SASIPHOTO/SHUTTERSTOCK ©

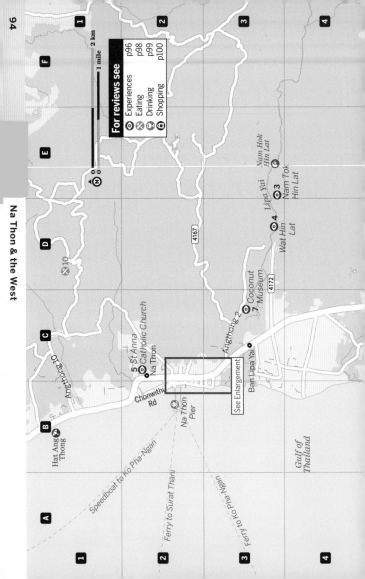

Na Thon & the West

For reviews see

	Experiences	p96
	Eating	p98
	Drinking	p99
	Shopping	p100

2 km
1 mile

Nam Hok
Hin Lat

Lipa Yai
3
Nam Tok
Hin Lat

4167

4
Wat Hin
Lat

4172

Coconut
7 Museum

Angthong 2

Ban Lipa Yai

5 St Anna
Catholic Church
Na Thon

See Enlargement

Chonwithi
Rd

Na Thon
Pier

Angthong Dr

10

Hat Ang
Thong

Gulf of
Thailand

Speedboat to Ko Pha-Ngan

Ferry to Surat Thani

Ferry to Ko Pha-Ngan

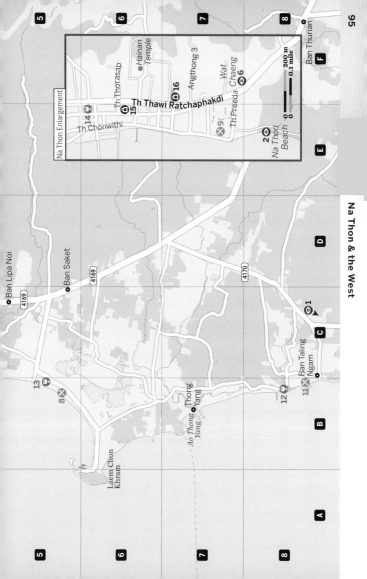

Na Thon & the West

Ban Thurian

Ban Lipa Noi

Ban Saket

4169

4169

4170

Ban Taling Ngam

Ao Thong Yang

Thong Yang

Laem Chon Khram

Na Thon Enlargement

Hainan Temple

Th Thorasap

Th Thawi Ratchaphakdi

Th Chonwithi

Angthong 3

Wat Chaeng

Th Preeda

Na Thon Beach

200 m
0.1 mile

Experiences

Ao Phang Ka   BEACH

1 MAP P94, C8

This lovely beach at the south-west corner of the island is even lovelier at low tide, when the water recedes to reveal a huge plateau of sand stretching to the horizon. Sunsets in summer are truly glorious (and snorkelling is good too, when the water's in), while the lack of tourist infrastructure means a castaway feel survives.

Na Thon Beach   BEACH

2 MAP P94, E8

When the tide is out, it's fun picking your way along the sand flats around Na Thon, especially south of the scrawnier beach near the pier. The sand flats widen

West Coast Sunsets

The west coast may be less visited than the east and north coasts, but visit towards the end of the day to catch the gulf burnished in the bronzes and golds of sunset that see the region come into its own. Excellent vantage points include Air Bar (p99), Five Islands (p98), Nikki Beach (p99), Ao Phang Ka (p96) and Na Thon Beach (p96), but almost anywhere will do.

out at low tide and you can find photogenic boats just sitting there – perfect at sunset.

Nam Tok Hin Lat   WATERFALL

3 MAP P94, E3

Near Na Thon, this waterfall is worth visiting if you've an afternoon to kill before taking a boat back to the mainland. After a mildly strenuous hike over streams and boulders, reward yourself with a dip in the pool at the bottom of the falls. Keep an eye out for the Buddhist temple that posts signs with spiritual words of moral guidance and enlightenment, but take sturdy shoes and water.

Wat Hin Lat   TEMPLE

4 MAP P94, D3

On the western part of Samui and near the waterfalls of the same name, this temple teaches daily *vipassana* meditation courses. (☏077 423146; admission free; ☉dawn-dusk)

St Anna Catholic Church   CHURCH

5 MAP P94, C2

This small green-tiled church off the 4169 across the way from the St Joseph School north of Na Thon is interesting as a Catholic outpost on the island, despite being a modern-build house of worship. The interior is simple, with paintings of the stations of the cross and a decorative floor. The church is open for mass on 6.30pm from Monday to Friday, at 7am on Saturday and at 8.30am on Sunday. (📞077 421149)

Wat Chaeng BUDDHIST TEMPLE

6 ◉ MAP P94, F7

This peaceful *wát* with a school attached is a place of quiet repose in the south of Na Thon. (admission free; 🕑dawn–dusk)

Coconut Museum MUSEUM

7 ◉ MAP P94, C3

This rather simple museum is very small and there are limited displays, but there's a lot of information to hand on the culture of coconuts on Ko Samui, including

Time & Tide

Due to its proximity to the equator, the tidal range in the Gulf of Thailand varies only slightly, often by no more than 3m. During the summer months, especially July and August, the tides are higher than in the winter, and the difference between low tide and high tide can vary by as little as 5cm, making it appear as if there is only one tide per day.

handy hints and tips on how to climb a coconut tree, if the urge takes you – you'll need a jute coil. (admission free)

Na Thon & the West Experiences

St Anna Catholic Church

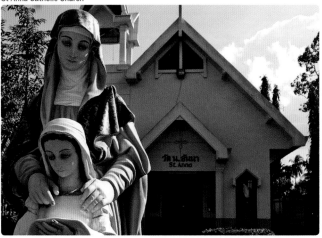

Hainan Temple

Fronted by a pair of golden Chinese lions and adorned with coiling dragons, this **temple** (Hailam Nathon Shrine; 海南公所; Map p94, C2; Na Thon; admission free; ☉dawn-dusk) is the most colourful Chinese temple (and guildhall) on the island. The shrine was set up by Thai-Chinese who originated from the island of Hăinán in the far south of China and is overseen by their descendants today, preserving a very local flavour and serving as a focal point for the community. You can find signs to the temple pointing off the 4169.

Eating

Big John's Seafood Restaurant
SEAFOOD $$

8 MAP P94, B5

This friendly restaurant is a popular west-coast seafood choice for sunset dining, with live evening entertainment. (☎077 485775; www.thelipa.com/bigjohn_restaurant. php; Lipa Noi; mains 150-300B; ☉8am-10pm; 🔊)

Lucky
INTERNATIONAL $$

9 🍽 MAP P94, E7

This restaurant facing the sea serves tasty and filling enough Western and Thai food, and it's convenient if you're off the boat or travelling up the west coast, but it's the sunset views and friendly service that nudge it into the recommended bracket. Good choice of vegetarian dishes too. (☎077 420392; Na Thon; dishes 100-250B; ☉8am-9pm Mon-Sat, noon-9pm Sun; 🔊)

Phootawan Restaurant
THAI $$

10 🍽 MAP P94, D1

Getting up the hill to this restaurant is a struggle on a scooter, but it's worth the effort to be rewarded with ranging, glorious views over the trees, rather than just for the serviceable food. To enjoy the visuals at their best, sunset is the time to arrive. (☎081 978 9241; mains from 150B; ☉9am-8.30pm)

Five Islands
SEAFOOD $$$

11 🍽 MAP P94, B8

Five Islands offers a unique (yet pricey) eating experience. First, a long-tail boat (tours for two including meal 7500B to 9250B) will take you out into the turquoise sea to visit the haunting Five Sister Islands where you'll learn about the ancient art of harvesting bird nests to make bird's-nest soup, a Chinese delicacy. When you return a deluxe meal is waiting for you on the beach.

Lunch tours departs around 9am, and the dinner programs leave around 3pm. Customers are also welcome to dine without going on the tour and vice versa but if you want the tour, book two days in advance. (📞 077 423577; www.thefiveislandssamui.com; Taling Ngam; dishes 250-620B; 🕐 11.30am-late)

Drinking

Air Bar   BAR

12 🍺 MAP P94, B8

Toast the setting sun as it sinks into the golden gulf from this magnificent outside bar perched above a cliff at this swanky resort (p143). There's an excellent menu of tapas and snacks if you simply can't pull yourself away

and want to make a meal of it. This is pretty much the top romantic choice on the island. (www.samui.intercontinental.com; Intercontinental Samui Baan Taling Ngam Resort, Taling Ngam; 🕐 5pm-midnight)

Nikki Beach   BAR

13 🍺 MAP P94, B5

The acclaimed luxury brand brings international flair to the secluded west coast of Ko Samui. Think haute cuisine, chic decor, gaggles of jet-setters and killer sunsets. Themed brunch and dinner specials keep the masses coming throughout the week, and sleek villa accommodation is also on offer. (📞 077 914500; www.nikkibeach.com/kohsamui; Lipa Noi; 🕐 11am-11pm; 📶)

Pàt tai

Max Murphys

BAR

14 🍸 MAP P94, E6

This fun Irish pub offers all the usual ingredients of a fun night: Premier League fixtures, Western and Thai pub grub, draught beer (Guinness, Kilkenny, Hoegaarden), a few craft beers, cocktails and obliging staff. It's as Irish as a bowl of tom yam soup, but after a few pints, you won't care. (46/1 Mu 3, Na Thon; ⏰9am-1am)

Shopping

Thanon An Thong

STREET

15 🔒 MAP P94, E6

Just a block inland from the pier, this pretty street is lined with wooden shophouses, Chinese lanterns and caged singing birds, with souvenir shops plying goods and gifts you can pick up more cheaply and with less pushing and shoving than in Chaweng.

Na Thon Day Market

MARKET

16 🔒 MAP P94, F7

The biggest and busiest of Samui's fresh markets; it also offers take-away food.

Fresh coconuts

Coconut Island

The definitive tree on Ko Samui, the coconut palm is not just a highly photogenic shape and a symbol of easygoing beach life, it's also a very important cash crop and one that has a deeply symbiotic relationship with the people of the island. Wherever you go on Ko Samui, you'll be greeted by the languorous, lilting form of coconut palms, their slender trunks reaching to the sky and fanning out into a fan of fronds. Husks litter the ground between trees and if you cycle around the south coast, you'll pass vast piles of harvested coconuts baking beneath the sun.

Resource-Rich Palms

Growing up to 30m in height, coconut palms thrive readily on warm, sandy soil and have developed a high tolerance for saline conditions; coupled with their love of sunlight, regular rainfall and high humidity, they are regularly found near the Ko Samui shoreline. The coconut and its palm are the source of many valuable resources, from coconut meat to cold-pressed virgin coconut oil (used in cooking for frying), coconut water, coconut milk (produced from the coconut kernel) and copra. You'll see many resorts employing palm fronds as a versatile and lightweight roofing material. The wood of the tree is also a valuable material for use in building, while the carved shell of the coconut is often used decoratively – you'll see them for sale along Chaweng Beach Rd, colourfully painted and glazed.

Cash Crop

With an estimated three million coconut palms on the island, coconuts are the second largest source of revenue on Ko Samui after tourism and until recently, the fruit was the island's main source of income. Each coconut palm produces around 70 coconuts annually and Ko Samui still provides Bangkok with over two million coconuts every month. Usually put on as a show for tourists, farmers occasionally still use pig-tailed macaques to climb trees to harvest coconuts (they can harvest up to 1000 of the fruit in one day). To find out more about coconuts and the role of the crop on the island, the modest Coconut Museum (p97) provides a simple introduction.

Top Experience 📷
Ang Thong Marine National Park

This chain of 40-odd jagged jungle islands stretches across the cerulean sea like a shattered emerald necklace – each featuring sheer limestone cliffs, hidden lagoons and perfect peach-coloured sands. The power of the seas has eroded the limestone to fashion dramatic arches, secret caves and lagoons and the panoramas that inspired Alex Garland's cult novel the Beach.

◉ adult/child 300/150B

Ko Wua Talap & Viewpoint

The largest island in the chain and home to the national park office and visitor bungalows, Ko Wua Talap has a stunning mountain-top viewpoint rewarding an arduous 450m trail that takes roughly an hour to complete – it might just be the most amazing vista in the whole of Thailand. From the top, sweeping views range to the jagged islands nearby as they burst through the placid turquoise waters.

Ko Mae Ko, Emerald Lagoon & Viewpoint

With an ethereal minty tint, the Emerald Lagoon (also called the Inner Sea) on Ko Mae Ko is a large lake in the middle of the island, fed by underwater channels, that spans an impressive 250m by 350m. You can look but you can't touch; the lagoon is strictly off limits to the unclean human body. A dramatic viewpoint can be found at the top of a series of staircases nearby.

Ko Samsao & Ko Tai Plao

The naturally occurring stone arches on Ko Samsao and Ko Tai Plao are visible during seasonal tides and weather conditions. Because the sea is quite shallow around the island chain, reaching a maximum depth of 10m, extensive coral reefs have not developed, except in a few protected pockets on the southwest and northeast sides. There's a shallow coral reef near Ko Tai Plao and Ko Samsao that has decent but not excellent snorkelling.

★ **Top Tips**

○ The best months to visit are February to April, when the seas are relatively calm.

○ It's too rough to visit in November and December, thanks to the monsoon rains.

○ Hikers should wear sturdy shoes.

🍴 **Take a Break**

There's a small restaurant at the park office, though food is often included on tours.

Getting There

Organised tours depart from Ko Samui and Ko Pha-Ngan, and include transport to/from the park, plus kayaking, snorkelling, hikes and lunch.

Explore ◈
Ko Pha-Ngan

This gulf isle offers much more than the Full Moon Parties that made it famous. Choose quieter days in the lunar calendar, or the smaller (but still raucous) half-moon party periods, and the island's charms are brought to the fore. It's easier to get a room, prices are more reasonable and far fewer people are on the island, meaning more solitude and tranquillity. Even Hat Rin – party central when the moon is round – is quiet and relaxing during other periods, and the beaches are kept clean.

There's a lot to explore on the island, so it pays to be selective. Breakfast at Nira's (p119) is always an excellent start to the day, but if you want to catch sunrise, ride a scooter to Hat Than Sadet (p115) on the east coast and pick your way over to Hat Thong Reng (p106). Consider hopping aboard a long-tail boat to Hat Khuat, or you can bounce over the waves south to Hat Rin, via Hat Thian. The Domsila Viewpoint (p113), on the hike above the waterfall at Nam Tok Phaeng (p113), is worth either a morning or afternoon of your time. For sunset libations head to the Secret Beach Bar (p121) or explore the brew sensations at the Belgian Beer Bar (p122).

Getting There & Around

As always, the cost and departure times for ferries are subject to change. Rough waves are sometimes known to cancel ferries between November and December.

Ko Pha-Ngan Map on p116

Long-tail boats, Ko Pha-Ngan DKART/GETTY IMAGES ©

Top Experience 📷
Ko Pha-Ngan's Hidden Beaches

Ko Pha-Ngan is fringed with delightful bays, inlets, coves and beaches and if you avoid the full-moon and half-moon shenanigans, you may even find them largely deserted. Even Sunrise Beach, transformed into an arena of sound during the Full Moon, is quiet for the rest of the month, but if you're willing to explore, you'll stumble upon some real gems.

 MAP P116, F4

Hat Thong Reng

The old-school beach charms of titchy **Hat Thong Reng** (Map p116, F5) allow you to rediscover the Ko Pha-Ngan of yesteryear. Whizz over to Hat Than Sadet on a scooter, cross the rickety bridge over the river in the south of the sands and clamber over the boulders by the Mai Pen Rai bungalows (watch your step, or walk over the hill) to this minute bay, fringed with swaying palms and sunk in solitude.

Hat Yao (East)

Not to be confused with Hat Yao on the north-west of the island, **Hat Yao** (Map p116, F5) is a secluded beach on the southeast coast, delight-fully fringed with white sand. There's no road ac-cess, so transport is either by long-tail boat from Hat Thian and Hat Yuan (which can be reached from Hat Rin), or on foot along the demanding four-hour, 7km-long mountain path from Hat Rin. If you trek it, take lots of water.

Hat Wai Nam

Like Hat Yao (East) around 1.5km to the north, **Hat Wai Nam** (Map p116, F6) is a white-sand beach that's also accessible on foot from Hat Rin along the path that meanders up the mountain. It's also reachable by long-tail boat from Hat Thian, Hat Yuan and Hat Rin. The reward is a secluded beach with gorgeous waters for dipping into.

Hat Thian

Site of the Sanctuary lodgings (p143) the beach of Hat Thian is an isolated stretch of sand cling-ing to the island's east coast. The beach has serious cachet among the backpacking fraternity and New Age crowd for its secluded vibe.

Hat Khuat

Commonly known as **Bottle Beach** (Map p116, D2; pictured), its inaccessibility helps it maintain a special allure; many visitors stay for several days or weeks at a time. You can trek here from Chalok Lam or hop aboard a long-tail boat.

★ **Top Tips**

○ If walking to any of these beaches, head off early in the morning to avoid the midday sun.

○ If returning on foot, give yourself enough time to avoid the dark, but pack a flashlight for emergencies.

○ Wear a light pair of long trousers if trek-king, to protect your legs from insects and plants.

✕ **Take a Break**

Hunger pangs? The restaurant at Mai Pen Rai (p143) is a good choice for keeping the munchies at bay, or sit down to some delicious, whole-some food at the Sanctuary (p121) at Hat Thian.

Top Experience
Full Moon Party

No one knows exactly when or how these crazy parties started – most believe they began in 1988, but accounts of the first party range from an Australian backpacker's going-away bash in August to hippies fleeing Samui's 'electric parties' in October. It matters little: today, thousands of bodies converge monthly on Sunrise Beach for an epic dusk-till-dawn trance-a-thon.

◎ MAP P116, E7

Hat Rin Nok

100B

☼ full moon, dusk–dawn

Sunrise Beach

Hat Rin Nok (aka Sunrise Beach; pictured) is the pounding heart of the full moon action; its kerosene-soaked sands see crowds swelling to an outrageous 40,000 party-goers during high season, while the low season still sees a respectable 8000 wide-eyed pilgrims.

Rock

With views over the fluorescent ocean of painted bodies high up above the swell of Hat Rin Nok, the **Rock** (☎093 725 7989; ⊙8am-late) is a perfectly placed bar to rest your sweaty limbs and get an elevated perspective on all things Full Moon. Chill out with a cocktail, while a decent menu provides the calories to get you through the night and soak up some of that excess alcohol.

Buckets, Buckets & More Buckets

You'll be knocking into stalls selling buckets of alcohol – vodka, gin, rum, whisky, mixed with coke and Red Bull – all along the beach, but go easy: you can quickly end up downing more than you think. Try to leave them till late.

Fire Ropes & Thumping Bass

Flaming among the thumping bass line and flashing neon are the petrol-drenched fire ropes where dancers are invited to hop over a swinging line of fire (burns are generally the order of the day on that one).

Accommodation

Have your accommodation sorted way up front – if you turn up on the day, you won't find a bed for the night in Hat Rin, though you can always do an in-and-out from Ko Samui.

★ **Top Tips**

○ Wear trainers or shoes, as there can be glass on the beach.

○ Don't drink and drive and don't go in the sea.

○ Fluorescent body paint won't come out of your clothes.

✕ **Take a Break**

Climb the north end of the beach to **Mellow Mountain** bar (⊙24hr; ☎), for an elevated perspective on the partying.

Walking Tour

Snacking Your Way Around Thong Sala

The best day to explore Thong Sala is Saturday during the Thong Sala Walking Street, when things are at their busiest best, but at other times, follow this walk to discover interesting cafes or to wander the lazy local back roads.

Walk Facts

Start Fat Cat
End Hub
Length 850m; 45-60mins, depending on how many stops you make

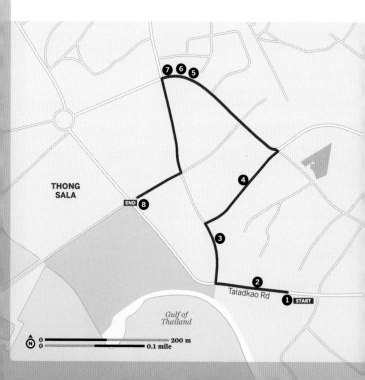

❶ Fat Cat

Start your day with a coffee at **Fat Cat** (breakfast from 70B; mains 90-195B; ⏰9am-3pm Mon-Sat; 📶) on Taladkao Rd, a charming spot at the heart of the settlement providing an excellent people-watching position on the street outside, which is stuffed during the Thong Sala Walking Street (p123).

❷ Chinese Shopfronts

Walk past old traditional shopfronts with wooden doors; many are shops owned by the Thai-Chinese, hence the red and gold Chinese couplets bestowing good fortune and fortuitous symbols, including *bagua* trigram mirrors to ward off the dispositions of evil and bad luck.

❸ Grab a Gelato

Turn the corner as Taladkao Rd bends right next to houses lined with potted plants and stop off at **Satimi** (per scoop 30-40B; ⏰10.30am-6.30pm Tue-Sun) to cool down with some excellent gelato or sorbets. There are several interesting shops here for you to browse in, too.

❹ Soi Phupattana Market Street

Soi Phupattana is a bustling, traditional market road where locals shop for fresh veggies, seafood, dried chilli and other herbs.

❺ Thong Sala Food Market

The food market (p119) is the hub of street food life in Thong Sala, a bustling galaxy of stalls that open in the early afternoon and steam on till around 11pm, serving everything from omelettes to curry, kebabs and spring rolls. It's always heaving, so sharpen your elbows and join in.

❻ Phantip Food Center

After exploring all the snacks on show at the food market, if you want a sit-down meal instead, head to the Phantip Food Center at the rear of the market, where delicious Thai staples await – take a seat at one of the communal tables.

❼ Dots Cafe

For smooth coffee, **Dots** (snacks from 60B; ⏰8.30am-9pm Mon-Sat, 9am-6pm Sun; 📶) is a perfect place for a latte or a cappuccino in trendy surrounds and an opportunity to relax. It also sells cool shades in wooden frames, natural creams, oils, clothes, candles and necklaces.

❽ A Pint at the Hub

To round off your day, have a pint of beer or a glass of wine at **Hub** (📞088 825 4158; ⏰8am-midnight; 📶), wander down to the seafront and bask in the sunset, watching local kids running around and playing football.

Walking Tour 🥾

Hiking to Domsila Viewpoint

This trail takes you past waterfalls and into the hills to the Domsila Viewpoint, which gazes out over the island. From the viewpoint you can either continue to follow the marked trail beyond the jungle, or head back the way you came. The waterfall and route opens at 8am and closes at 5pm. Take good, strong shoes and lots of water. Look out for loose rocks.

Walk Facts

Start Visitor Centre

End Domsila Viewpoint

Distance 700m; 45 minutes

❶ Visitor Centre

From Thong Sala, follow the 6038 road for around 4km till you see the brown sign for the Thansadej-Koh Pang-an National Park and then turn right along to the visitor centre/national park office, a short journey from the turn-off. Note the map of the Nam Tok Phaeng-Dom Sila Nature Trail on the board, and take a photo of it for reference.

❷ Phaeng Nai Waterfall

Around 100m from the start of the trail, this is the first waterfall you come to, gushing in the wetter months with a pool at the bottom, where you can go for a swim if there's enough water. You may see local kids frolicking around in the cool liquid.

❸ Phaeng Yai Waterfall

Beyond lies the Phaeng Yai Waterall – which varies in intensity like all falls depending on the rainy season – and the climb proper begins up to the Domsila Viewpoint. There's a pool here too for splashing about in. Set off up the hill, watching out for roots crossing the path through the jungle. Look around at the various trees around you – this is part of the Koh Pha-Ngan National Park.

❹ Than Nam Rak Waterfall & Kahn Ban Dai Waterfall

This signposted waterfall around 200m up the hill has a lovely plunge pool and is gorgeous during the wet season. Follow the ropes to a further waterfall, Kahn Ban Dai Waterfall, which is further along.

❺ Than Song Praeng & Than Klouy Mai Waterfalls

Further along gush these two falls – for the Than Song Praeng waterfall, there's a rope to pull yourself up to it. Beyond the falls is a branch in the road – turn left and keep going downhill till you reach the Domsila Viewpoint.

❻ Domsila Viewpoint

Rewarding your climb, these rocks are an astonishing **vantage point** (Map p116, C4) with views ranging over Ko Pha-Ngan and off to Ang Thong Marine Park and Ko Samui. You can backtrack to the fork in the road to keep going along the nature trail which continues in a long loop before returning to Phaeng Yai Waterfall or Phaeng Nai Waterfall. but this takes several hours. Alternatively, head back down the way you came.

Motorbike Tour 🛵

Ban Tai to Hat Thong Reng

This terrific scooter, motorbike or bicycle journey takes you from Ban Tai to the gorgeous beach at Hat Thong Reng, to explore Thai temples, a traditional village, and the heart of Ko Pha-Ngan's jungle interior before plunging down to the sea, past waterfalls, to an azure bay pinched between rocky headlands.

Route Facts

Start Wat Pho, Ban Tai

End Hat Thong Reng

Length 11km; 90 minutes by motorbike, including stops

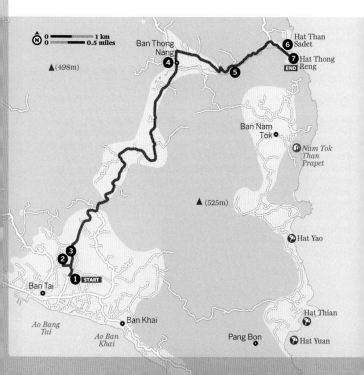

❶ Wat Pho

At the 7-Eleven in Ban Tai you'll see a sign pointing to Thong Nai Pan Beach (13.5km) leading you north along the 2079. **Wat Pho** (admission free; ☺dawn-dusk), with its imposing gateway, has large grounds and a herbal sauna opposite.

❷ Ko Pha-Ngan's Tallest Yang Na Yai Tree

This terrific tree seems to poke into the Ko Pha-Ngan clouds. Garlanded with ribbons, it's encircled by a protective balustrade with a small information board explaining the tree's significance.

❸ Ban Nok

The small village of Ban Nok has a diminutive temple that peeks from the foliage along the signposted dirt path beyond the tree. Though the temple is a very simple one-hall affair and very easy to miss, the village around it offers glimpses of traditional Thai life, a million miles from the coastal settlements that revolve around tourism. Return to the fork in the road by the Yang Na Yai Tree and turn right to continue along the 2079.

❹ Big Bang Art Cafe

Continue for around 6km as the road climbs steeply into the dense jungle interior of the island. Just before you reach the roundabout, look out for the **Big Bang Art Cafe** (☎098 431 2754; mains 60-220B; ☺10am-6pm) up the steps on your left, run by a Swiss graphic designer and his local wife.

❺ Deang Waterfall

Turn right at the roundabout and zip down towards Hat Than Sadet. There's a string of falls here, leading to the sea, but the best is Deang Waterfall. Explore at will; if the water is in full spate, it's quite a sight.

❻ Hat Than Sadet

This lovely white-sand **beach** (Map p116, F4) is beyond the palms, so park your scooter and wander along the sands. Hat Than Sadet still has a rather isolated feel, despite the road now running all the way to it.

❼ Hat Thong Reng

Cross the bridge over the river at the south end to the Mai Pen Rai bungalows – taking a look upriver – and consider clambering around the rocks to the beach of **Hat Thong Reng** (Map p116, F4). If you find it too hard going, just sit on the rocks and gaze out to sea.

Ko Pha-Ngan

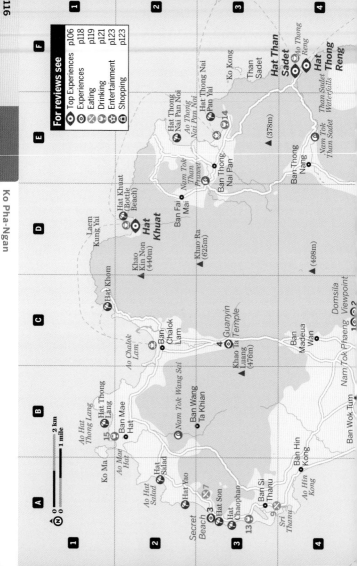

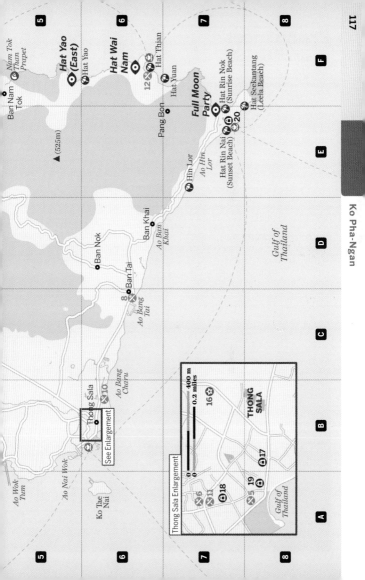

Ko Pha-Ngan

5
Nam Tok Than Prapet
Ban Nam Tok
Hat Yao (East)
Hat Yao

6
Hat Wai Nam
Hat Thian
12
Hat Yuan
Pang Bon
▲(525m)

7
Full Moon Party
Hat Rin Nok (Sunrise Beach)
20
Hat Rin Nai (Sunset Beach)
Him Lor
Ao Him Lor

8
Hat Seekantang (Leela Beach)
Gulf of Thailand

F
E
D
C

Ban Nam Tok
Ban Nok
Ban Khai
Ao Ban Khai
Ban Tai
8
Ao Bang Tai
Thong Sala
10
Ao Bang Charu
See Enlargement

Ao Wok Tham
Ao Nai Wok
Ko Tae Nai

Thong Sala Enlargement

0   400 m
0   0.2 miles

16
THONG SALA
17
18
6
11
19
5
Gulf of Thailand

A
B

Experiences

Domsila Viewpoint VIEWPOINT

1 ◉ MAP P116, C4

The terrific Domsila Viewpoint – offering a rocky perch with superb, ranging views – is a 15-minute, root-choked climb up from Nam Tok Phaeng waterfall. Then you can either backtrack or continue on the two- to three-hour trail through the jungle in a loop, past other waterfalls before bringing you back. Take water and good shoes.

Nam Tok Phaeng WATERFALL

2 ◉ MAP P116, C4

Nam Tok Phaeng is protected by a national park; this waterfall is a pleasant reward after a short but rough hike. After the waterfall (dry out of season), it's a further exhilarating 15-minute climb up a root-choked path (along the Phaeng-Domsila Nature Trail) to the fantastic Domsila Viewpoint, with superb, ranging views. The two- to three-hour trail then continues on through the jungle in a loop, past other waterfalls before bringing you back. Take water and good shoes.

Secret Beach BEACH

3 ◉ MAP P116, A3

Not so secret, this palm-fringed, soft-sand cove (aka Hat Son) down a steep road in the northwest of the island is a gorgeous choice for sunset, but any time of day will do. To fully get in the mood, check into the **Haad Son Resort** (☏077

Guanyin Temple

DANIEL MACHACEK/SHUTTERSTOCK ©

349104; www.haadsonresort.net; bungalows 1875-6750B; ❄ @ 🛜 🏊), or sink a twilight cocktail at the Secret Beach Bar (p121). Swimming here is generally very good.

Guanyin Temple
BUDDHIST TEMPLE

4 ◉ MAP P116, C3

Signposted as the 'Goddess of Mercy Shrine Joss House', this fascinating Chinese temple is dedicated to Guanyin, the Buddhist Goddess of Mercy. The temple's Chinese name (普岳山) on the entrance gate refers to the island in China that is the legendary home of the goddess. The main hall – the Great Treasure Hall – is a highly colourful confection, containing several bodhisattvas, including Puxian (seated on an elephant) and Wenshu (sitting on a lion).

Look out for the statue of a 1000-hand Guanyin, housed in the Guanyin Palace. The admission price is supposedly a voluntary donation. (40B; ⏲7am-6pm)

Wake Up
WATER SPORTS

Jamie passes along his infinite wakeboarding wisdom to eager wannabes at his small water sports school in Chalok Lam. Fifteen minutes of 'air time' will set you back 1200B, which is excellent value considering you get one-on-one instruction. Kneeboarding, wakeskating, wakesurfing and waterskiing sessions are also available. (📞087 283 6755; www.wakeupwakeboarding.com; from 1200B; ⏲Jan-Oct)

Doing the Laundry

If you got fluorescent body paint on your clothes during your full moon romp, don't bother sending them to the cleaners – it will never come out. Trust us, we've tried. For your other washing needs, there are heaps of places that will gladly wash your clothes. Prices hover around 40B per kilo, and express cleanings shouldn't be more than 60B per kilo.

Eating

Nira's
BAKERY $

5 ✗ MAP P116, A8

With lots of busy staff offering outstanding service, a big and bright interconnected two-room interior, scrummy baked goodies, tip-top coffee (and exotic rarities such as Marmite and Vegemite) and trendy furniture, Nira's is second to none in Thong Sala, and perhaps the entire island. This is *the* place for breakfast. Music is cool, jazzy chillout. (Thong Sala; snacks from 80B; ⏲7am-7pm; 🛜)

Thong Sala Food Market
MARKET $

6 ✗ MAP P116, A7

A heady mix of steam and snacking locals, Thong Sala's terrific

Beware the Box Jellyfish

There are several species of venomous jellyfish in the waters off Ko Pha-Ngan, Ko Samui and Ko Tao, including scyphozoans, hydrozoans and box jellyfish. The most notorious is the box jellyfish, a cnidarian invertebrate whose sting – which contains a potent venom that attacks the nervous system, heart and skin cells – can result in death. Growing up to 3m in length and named after the box-like appearance of its bell, the box jellyfish's sting can be so painful the swimmer can enter a state of shock and drown before reaching the shore. The jellyfish is more prolific in sea waters after heavy rain.

Ko Pha-Ngan and Ko Samui have the highest incidence of fatal and near-fatal box jellyfish stings in the whole of Thailand. Some beaches, such as Hat Rin Nok, are equipped with stations warning of the danger of jellyfish, as well as providing a cylinder containing standard household vinegar, which should be poured onto the area affected by the sting for 30 seconds. Avoid the inclination to rub or scratch the stung area.

food market is a must for those looking for doses of culture while nibbling on low-priced snacks. Wander the stalls for a galaxy of Thai street food, from vegetable curry puffs to corn on the cob, spicy sausages, kebabs, spring rolls, Hainanese chicken rice or coconut ice cream. There's a sit-down section at the rear, served by a number of Thai kitchens, as well as a few Italian ones and a vegetarian option. (Thong Sala; dishes 25-180B; ⏱1-11pm)

Bubba's Coffee Bar
CAFE $

Bubba's is a superb caffeination choice on the north side of the road between Thong Sala and Hat Rin (see 8 Ⓧ Map p116, C6). Pull in,

find a seat, relax and enjoy some fine coffee and the easy-going atmosphere (despite attracting legions of customers from the nearby hostels). The wholesome menu is lovely too, as is the cool interior. (Ban Tai; mains 120-220B; ⏱7am-5pm; 📶)

Pura Vida
CAFE $

7 Ⓧ MAP P116, A3

Hobbled only by short opening hours, this charming and bright Portuguese cafe is an alluring choice as you head up the west coast. Breakfasts are excellent, especially the pancakes and natural yoghurt, but you can go the whole hog with a full brekkie, and delicious burgers, sandwiches and paninis are also served. Love the

'Eat Well, Travel Often' campervan painting. (☑095 034 9372; Hat Yao; mains from 120B; ⏰8.30am-3pm Mon-Sat)

Fisherman's Restaurant

SEAFOOD $$

8 MAP P116, C6

Sit in a long-tail boat looking out over the sunset and a rocky pier. Lit up at night, it's one of the island's nicest settings, and the food, from the addictive yellow-curry crab to the massive seafood platter to share, is as wonderful as the ambience. Reserve ahead, especially when the island is hopping during party time. (☑084 454 7240; Ban Tai; dishes 50-600B; ⏰1.30-10pm)

Crave

BURGERS $$

9 MAP P116, A3

Attractively bedecked with glowing lanterns at night, this excellent, very popular and atmospheric choice in Sri Thanu puts together some fine burgers in a cosy and charming setting. Cocktails are great too, starting at 170B. Shame it's only open evenings. (☑098 838 7268; www.cravekohphangan.com; Sri Thanu; mains from 200B; ⏰6-10pm Wed-Mon; 🛜)

Ando Loco

MEXICAN $

10 MAP P116, B6

This superpopular outdoor Mexican hang-out still gets the universal thumbs-up. Grab a jumbo margarita, down a 'drunken fajita', line up a quesadilla or two and sink a round of balls on the pool table with a tequila or two to go with it. (☑085 791 7600; www.andoloco.com; Ban Tai; mains from 50B; ⏰1-10pm Wed-Mon)

SOHO

BURGERS $$

11 MAP P116, A7

This terrific British-run burger restaurant is modern, stylish, spacious, welcoming, efficient, at the hub of Thong Sala life and a breath of fresh air. The burgers are fabulously juicy and a cut above the rest, while it's also a superb place for a pint as it doubles as a flash bar. (Thong Sala; mains from 180B; ⏰9.30am-midnight)

Sanctuary

HEALTH FOOD $$

12 MAP P116, F6

The restaurant at the Sanctuary resort (p143) proves that wholesome food (vegetarian and seafood) can also be delicious. Enjoy a tasty parade of plates – from massaman curry to crunchy Vietnamese spring rolls. Don't forget to wash it all down with a blackberry, soy milk and honey immune booster. No credit cards. (www.thesanctuarythailand.com; Hat Thian; mains from 130B; 🛜)

Drinking

Secret Beach Bar

BAR

There are few better ways to unwind at the end of a Ko Pha-Ngan day than watching the sun slide into an azure sea from this bar on the northwest sands of the island (see 3 Map p116, A3). Grab a table, order a mojito and take in the sunset through the palm fronds. (Hat Son; ☺9am-7pm)

Belgian Beer Bar BAR

13 🚇 MAP P116, A3

Run by the affable Quentin, this enjoyable bar defies Surat Thani's appropriation by yogis and the chakra-balancing crowd with a heady range of Belgian beer, the most potent of which (Amber Bush) delivers a dizzying 12.5% punch. If the yogic flying doesn't give you wings, this might. (www.seetanu.com; Ban Sri Thanu; ☺8am-10pm)

Flip Flop Pharmacy BAR

14 🚇 MAP P116, E3

With flip-flops on the wall, this popular beach bar on the sands of Thong Nai Pan has a fine beach perspective (and pool table) and a terrific setting. (Thong Nai Pan; ☺noon-1am; 🛜)

Three Sixty Bar BAR

15 🚇 MAP P116, B1

High up a road east of Ko Ma, the Three Sixty Bar does what it says on the packet, with splendid, wide-angle views – sunset time is killer. (Ban Mae Hat; ☺8am-midnight)

Hat Rin Nok (p109)

PETER UNGER/GETTY IMAGES ©

Entertainment

Moonlight Cinema
CINEMA

16 ⭐ MAP P116, B7

Set in a seductive garden/jungle setting, this cosy cinema – the only one on the island – has a huge screen, great smoothies, a bar, fantastic vegan food and some excellent films (with headphones provided). It's fun, atmospheric and highly relaxing. (☑093 638 5051; www.moonlightphangan.com; Thong Sala; 150B; ⏱3pm-1am Tue-Fri, 1pm-1am Sat & Sun; 🛜)

Shopping

Thong Sala Walking Street
MARKET

17 🔒 MAP P116, B8

Thong Sala's Walking Street market kicks off every Saturday from around 4pm, with a terrific choice of street food, souvenirs, gifts, handicrafts and clothes. It's the best time to see Thong Sala at its liveliest. (Taladkao Rd, Thong Sala; ⏱4-10pm Sat)

Lilawadee
CLOTHING

18 🔒 MAP P116, A7

This neat and idiosyncratic shop stocks a sparkling range of customised, head-turning glitter motorbike helmets, stacked temptingly on shelves at the rear, fashion, art and clothing. If it's raining, expect hours to be reduced to noon to 8pm. (☑630 920327; Thong Sala; ⏱10.30am-1.30pm & 5-9pm Fri-Wed)

Phanganer
CLOTHING

19 🔒 MAP P116, A8

At the southern end of Thong Sala's Walking Street near the bend towards the sea, this small clothing shop has a cool and colourful selection of shirts (from 290B), T-shirts, cargo shorts (690B), belts and wallets. (Thong Sala; ⏱10am-7pm)

Fusion Fashion
CLOTHING

20 🔒 MAP P116, E7

There's sadly not a great deal of worthwhile shopping choice in Hat Rin, but this small boutique is worth stopping by for its attractive and eye-catching line of boho and colourful gossamer blouses, skirts, hot pants, bags and jewellery. (Hat Rin; ⏱11am-10pm)

Explore ⊛

Ko Tao

This jungle-topped cutie has the busy vibe of Samui mixed with the laid-back nature of Pha-Ngan. Hikers and hermits can re-enact an episode from Lost in the dripping coastal jungles, and when you're Robinson Crusoe-ed out, hit the pumpin' bar scene that rages on until dawn. But Tao also has a wild card: accessible, diverse diving right off its shores.

After breakfast (p136) in Sairee Village or Mae Hat, hike or hop aboard a scooter to Ao Tanot (p130) to enjoy the dawn sun from the sands of this bay on the east coast, where you can snorkel or leap into the azure waters from the huge rock in the bay. Head back to Sairee Beach via the West Coast Viewpoint (p126), before trekking south around the coast from Mae Hat to Ao Chalok Ban Kao. For dinner, return to Mae Hat to select from one of its fantastic dining choices (p136). Come dusk there's only one place to be – sinking into a beach-side beanbag on the west coast, or choosing from one of the other viewpoints with a vantage point out onto the setting sun (p126).

Getting There & Around

Costs and departure times are subject to change. Rough waves are known to cancel ferries between October and December. When the waters are choppy we recommend taking the Seatran rather than the Lomprayah catamaran if you are prone to seasickness. (The catamarans ride the swell, whereas the Seatran cuts through the currents.) Note that we highly advise purchasing your boat tickets *several* days in advance if you are accessing Ko Tao from Ko Pha-Ngan after the Full Moon Party.

Ko Tao Map on p132

Top Experience
West Coast Sunsets

With much of the island action and bars cluster-
ing in a long strip along the middle of the west
coast, there's no shortage of places to view the
sunset from Ko Tao with cocktail in hand, but
it pays to pick and choose, so you get the best,
most comfortable and most idyllic perspective
(preferably from the comfort of a beachside
beanbag).

◎ MAP P132, D5

Fizz

Come sundown, grab a beer or a cocktail and sink into one of **Fizz's** (Map p132, C4; Sairee Beach; ☺8am-1am) green beanbags for a ringside view of the setting sun. With the lapping of the waves and ambient sounds, it's a glorious conclusion to the day and there's little reason or incentive to move, especially when the candles are lit.

West Coast Viewpoint

This superb viewpoint in the middle of the island affords glorious views of the west and northwest of the island from near two large boulders called Two View Rock. Head up along Sairee Soi 1 (look for the sign to OK View) to a fork in the road and head west for a short walk to the viewpoint. From the fork in the road, you can head down to Ao Tanot on the east coast, via the reservoir.

Nang Yuan Viewpoint

This **terrace** (Map p132, B2) across from Ko Nang Yuan in the northwest of the island is a superb spot to catch the sunset over the islands. It's located within the Dusit Buncha Resort (www.dusitbuncharesort.com), so if you want to make a meal of it, dine at the resort's restaurant.

Maya Beach Club

Rivalling Fizz as the top sunset bar on the west coast, **Maya** (Map p132, C5; ☎080 578 2225; www.mayabeachclubkohtao.com; Sairee Beach; ☺noon-9pm Sat-Thu, to 2am Fri) has a fine selection of cocktails to raise to your sensational blood-orange sunset from the comfort of your lounger. As the sea goes a terrific gold, the views are accompanied by nightly DJs playing super-chilled beats. You won't want to leave.

★ Top Tips

● Check on the weather report for sunset a few days up front and plan ahead.

● If choosing a bar, arrive early for the best seats/bean-bags/loungers.

● For the best sunsets, avoid the rainy season, though rain and sunsets can make for sublime photos.

✕ Take a Break

Tie in your sunset-watching duties with a drink at Fizz or Maya Beach Club, while **Fishbowl Beach Bar** (☎062 046 8996; Sairee Beach; ☺noon-2am) is a great place for live music and has awesome sunset views, too.

Top Experience 📷
Diving off Ko Tao

Ko Tao has some of the most supreme diving in Thailand, with an abundance of sites, from offshore pinnacles to shallow, sandy bays and wrecks, where aquamarine waters teem with marine life, including coral. It's also an excellent place to learn to dive, whether scuba diving or plunging down to the dark blue depths on a single breath-hold (freediving).

 MAP P132, A1

Chumphon Pinnacle

With a maximum diving depth of 36m and consisting of one large underwater pinnacle and several smaller ones, this is the most famous dive site near the island. It's also quite a challenge, so it's not for newbies. Being quite far offshore, a wide variety of aquatic life noses about the rock formations, making it a fascinating choice to see a diversity of sea life, including whale sharks.

Sail Rock

Poking from the sea between Ko Tao and Ko Pha-Ngan, **Sail Rock** (Map p132, F8) is around 90 minutes from Ko Tao so is done as a day trip. Its distance from the islands means marine life here is plentiful in its briny depths: expect to bump into giant grouper, batfish, barracuda, moral eels and bull sharks. Sail Rock's trump card is its 'chimney', a vertical swim through. Good for both the experienced and relative novices.

Southwest Pinnacle

With a maximum diving depth of 28m and located around 7km southwest of Ko Tao, this collection of **pinnacles** (Map p132, A8) is good for both experienced scuba divers and aquatic greenhorns. A magnificent profusion of marine life darts in and out of the pinnacles and gullies, so you can expect to see scorpionfish, barracuda and occasional whale sharks as well as delicate harp coral.

HTMS Sattakut

At a depth of 30m, this **vessel** (Map p132, B4; pictured), which once participated in the Battle of Iwo Jima as a US Navy ship, was deliberately sunk in 2011 to create an artificial reef and has become one of the most popular dive sites off Ko Tao. Considered a more advanced dive site, the wreck sits on the sand, with visiting groupers, snappers, wrasse, yellow barracudas, butterfly fish and rabbitfish.

★ **Top Tip**

○ Take some time to compare dive schools on the island and talk to others, weighing up your options before signing up.

✕ **Take a Break**

All breaks are held on dive boats, where food is provided.

Top Experience

Ao Tanot

The delightful curve of Ao Tanot stretches 200m along the mid-east side of the island and is bathed in golden sunrises. Reaching it is not hard, but the location lends the sheltered bay an alluring sense of seclusion. Five bungalow/resort operations are at hand if you want to stay, while restaurants serve beach-goers, sunseekers, snorkellers and divers.

◉ MAP P132, E5

Snorkelling & Swimming

With shallow and crystal waters and plenty of aquatic life and coral (which starts at a depth of 2m), Ao Tanot is supreme snorkelling territory, so pack a snorkel or hire one from one of the resorts (mask and snorkel usually between 50B and 100B). The waters are also rarely busy, so there's usually enough space to explore without interruption and get a clear sub-aqua view. If snorkelling, take extra care of the fragile corals and never stand on them.

Rock Jumping & Climbing

A huge and easily reached rock in the bay provides the ideal platform for spirited leaps into the sea, which is deep enough to accommodate plunges. Also go for a clamber over the rocks in the north of the bay by the Family Tanote bungalows – the views are serene, but put on loads of sunscreen.

Calypso Diving

This **dive operator** (☏ 077 456745; www.calypso-diving-kohtao.de; Ao Tanot) just off the beach offers a whole range of watery exploration, including fun dives – as well as night dives – in the waters of Ao Tanot and beyond. Calypso can also provide snorkelling gear.

Trek to Ao Tanot

You can get here by scooter, but it's more fun to explore the island by trekking the 4.5km from Sairee Beach. The cross-island trek via the West Coast Viewpoint (p126) leads up the road just south of Monsoon Gym. Follow this road and a dirt trail to a fork in the road named Two Views (turn left here to get to the viewpoint, for splendid panoramas over the west of the island), and head right via the reservoir and on down to Ao Tanot. The whole trip to is around 4.5km and takes around 90 minutes.

★ **Top Tip**

○ Consider staying overnight as it's very quiet and the sunrise is gorgeous.

✖ **Take a Break**

Head to **Poseidon** (☏ 077 456735; poseidonkohtao@ hotmail.com; 🛜) for a milkshake or a bite to eat, or climb up to the restaurant at **Family Tanote** (☏ 077 456757; ❄ @ 🛜) for fine views.

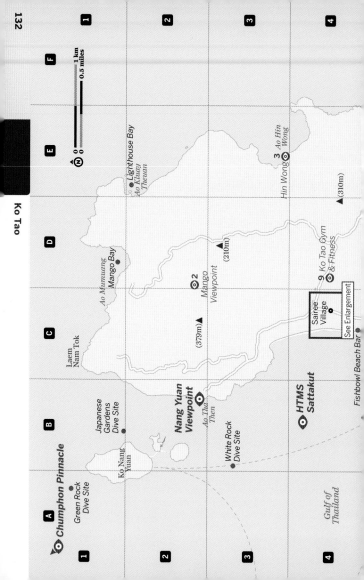

Ko Tao

Chumphon Pinnacle

Green Rock Dive Site

Ko Nang Yuan

Japanese Gardens Dive Site

Laem Nam Tok

Ao Mumuang Mango Bay

Lighthouse Bay

Ao Kluay Theuan

1 km
0.5 miles

N

Ao Hin Wong

3 Ao Hin Wong

Hin Wong

(310m)

Mango Viewpoint

2

(210m)

(379m)

9 Ko Tao Gym & Fitness

Nang Yuan Viewpoint

Ao Tha Then

White Rock Dive Site

Sairee Village

See Enlargement

HTMS Sattakut

Fishbowl Beach Bar

Gulf of Thailand

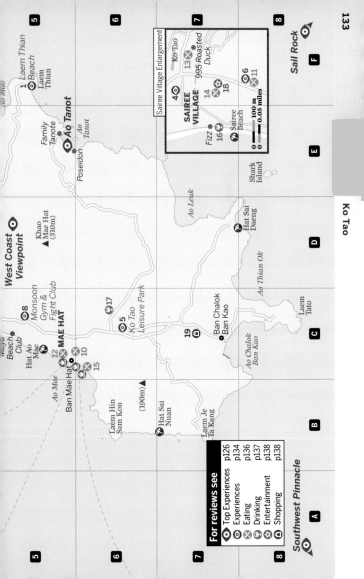

Ko Tao

5 | **6** | **7** | **8**

Laem Thian
1 Laem Thian Beach
Laem Thian

Family Tanote
Ao Tanot
Ao Tanot
Poseidon

Sairee Village Enlargement

Ko Tao
13 995 Roasted Duck
4
SAIREE VILLAGE
14
18
6
11

Fizz
16
Sairee Beach

0   100 m
0   0.05 miles

Shark Island

West Coast Viewpoint

Khao Mae Hat (310m)
Ao Leuk

Hat Sai Daeng

Sail Rock

Monsoon Gym & Fight Club
8
MAE HAT
Moya Beach Club
Hat Ao Mae
12
Ban Mae Hat
10
15

17

5 Ko Tao Leisure Park

Ban Chalok Ban Kao
19

Ao Chalok Ban Kao

Ao Thian Ok

Laem Tato

Laem Hin Sam Kon

Hat Sai Nuan
(190m)

Laem Je Ta Kang

A | **B** | **C** | **D** | **E** | **F**

Southwest Pinnacle

For reviews see	
Top Experiences	p126
Experiences	p134
Eating	p136
Drinking	p137
Entertainment	p138
Shopping	p138

Experiences

Laem Thian Beach
BEACH

1 ◉ MAP P132, F5

In the lee of the headland, this secluded and sheltered little white-sand beach in the middle of the east coast, north of Ao Tanot, is a delightful place with excellent snorkelling, fabulous rock jumping and very clear waters. It's quite a hike to get here along a dirt track; otherwise it's reachable by long-tail boat. There's the shell of an old resort here, crumbling away and covered in graffiti. If you hike, take loads of water and sunscreen.

The 2.5km walk from Sairee Village takes just over an hour.

Mango Viewpoint
VIEWPOINT

2 ◉ MAP P132, D2

With glorious views from up high, this viewpoint can be reached by motorbike – it's a tough journey and not safe on two wheels – but it's more fun to hike up and you can appreciate the climb. It's about an hour's climb up from Sairee Village, but the views are worth it. There are several places where you can get a drink on the way up, but it's a good idea to pack some water anyway. (100B)

Hin Wong
BAY

3 ◉ MAP P132, E3

This lovely bay on the east of the island across from Sairee Beach is boulder-strewn and the water is beautifully clear with excellent snorkelling. The road here has sudden holes and pits and is steep, so consider walking, which makes for an enjoyable and energetic trek; if you take a motorbike, be careful and if you're in doubt, always err on the side of caution.

Roctopus Dive
DIVING

4 ◉ MAP P132, F7

Centrally located on Sairee Beach, with great staff and high standards, this popular and bubbly dive school is a well-equipped, excellent choice for divers of all abilities. Choose from a half-day Try Dive and Open Water course for novices to speciality and advanced dive courses. It also runs a dedicated speedboat for snorkel trips, cliff jumping and private charters. (📞 077 456611, 090 863 1836; www. roctopusdive.com; Sairee Village; from 2100B)

Ko Tao Leisure Park
BOWLING, MINIGOLF

5 ◉ MAP P132, C6

On the main road between Mae Hat and Chalok Ban Kao, this place has homemade bowling lanes where the employees reset the pins after every frame (300B per hour). The 18-hole minigolf course has a landmark theme – putt your ball through Stonehenge or across the Golden Gate Bridge. There are also *pétanque* courts, table tennis and a big outdoor screen.

It's floodlit come nightfall. (📞 077 456316; ⏲ noon-midnight)

Flying Trapeze Adventures ACROBATICS

6 ⊙ MAP P132, F8

Test your vertigo and find if you're a great catch with a fun 90-minute small-group beginner trapeze lesson (1500B). Courses are taught by a superfriendly posse of limber sidekicks, who take you from circus neophyte to soaring savant in four jumps or fewer. There are occasional nightly shows, involving audience participation. Class times vary depending on sundown; reserve ahead. (FTA; 📞080 696 9269; www.goodtimethailand.com; Sairee Beach; ⏱4-8pm, lessons 3.30-5.30pm)

Goodtime Adventures HIKING, ADVENTURE SPORTS

7 ⊙ MAP P132, C4

Dive, hike through the island's jungle interior, swing from rock to rock during a climbing and abseiling session, or unleash your inner daredevil cliff-jumping or throwing yourself into multisport or power-boat handling. Alternatively, take a shot at all of them on the full-day Koh Tao Adventure (3300B).

The Goodtime office has its own cafe and and bar along the Sairee sands and also operates a hostel, with dorms and doubles. (📞087 275 3604; www.gtadventures.com; Sairee Beach; ⏱noon-late)

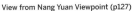

View from Nang Yuan Viewpoint (p127)

Dengue Fever

Be aware that mosquito-borne dengue fever is a real and serious threat on Ko Tao. The virus can spread quickly due to tightly packed tourist areas and the small size of the island. There is currently no widely available vaccine for dengue. The best precaution is to avoid being bitten by mosquitoes: use insect repellent and wear loose but protective clothing.

Monsoon Gym & Fight Club
MARTIAL ARTS

8 ◉ MAP P132, C5

This popular club combines *moo·ay tai* (Thai boxing) programs and air-con dorm accommodation (300B) for students signed up to get to grips with the fighting art. It's an excellent and exhilarating way to spend time in Ko Tao, if diving isn't your scene. The well-equipped concrete gym is right alongside the Thai boxing ring. Drop-in fight training costs 300B, six sessions is 1500B and monthly unlimited use is 7000B. (📞086 271 2212; www.monsoongym.com; Sairee Beach)

Ko Tao Gym & Fitness
GYM

9 ◉ MAP P132, D4

This well-equipped two-floor gym up the road from Sairee Village is

an excellent place for varying your exercise regime, with everything you might need to burn off some of those Ko Pha-Ngan acquired calories. (📞082 801 4014; www.kohtaogym.com; Sairee Village; 200B; ⏱7.30am-10pm Mon-Fri, 8am-9pm Sat & Sun)

Eating

Zest Coffee Lounge
CAFE $

10 ✖ MAP P132, C5

All brick and wood with a scuffed floor, Zest pulls out the stops to brew up some excellent coffee and wake up sleepyheads at brek-kie time. Eggs Benedict gets the morning off on the right foot, while idlers and snackers can nibble on ciabatta sandwiches or sticky confections while nursing their creamy caffe latte. There's a second branch in Sairee (open 8am to 5pm), although we prefer this location. (Mae Hat; dishes 70-200B; ⏱6am-4pm; 🛜)

Bang Burgers
BURGERS $

11 ✖ MAP P132, F8

You may have to dig your heels in and wait in line at this terrific burger bar that does a roaring trade in Sairee. There's around a half-dozen burgers (cheese, double cheese, red chilli cheese) on the menu, including a vegie choice for meat-free diners; chips are 50B. (📞081 136 6576; Sairee Village; mains from 130B; ⏱10am-10pm)

Pranee's Kitchen

THAI $

12 MAP P132, C5

An old Mae Hat fave, Pranee's serves scrumptious curries and other Thai treats in an open-air pavilion sprinkled with lounging pillows, wooden tables and TVs. English-language movies are shown nightly at 6pm. (Mae Hat; dishes 50-150B; ⏰7am-10pm; 📶)

The Gallery

THAI $$

13 MAP P132, F7

One of the most pleasant settings in town, the food here is equally special. The signature dish is *hor mok maprao on* (chicken, shrimp and fish curry served in a young coconut) but the white snapper fillet in creamy red curry sauce is also excellent and there's a choice of vegetarian dishes. (☎077 456547; www.thegallerykohtao.com; Sairee Village; mains 120-420B; ⏰noon-10pm)

Barracuda Restaurant & Bar

FUSION $$

14 MAP P132, F7

Sociable chef Ed Jones caters for the Thai princess when she's in town, but you can sample his exquisite cuisine for mere pennies in comparison to her budget. Locally sourced ingredients are turned into creative, fresh, fusion masterpieces. Try the seafood platter, pan-fried barracuda fillet or vegetarian falafel platter – then wash it down with a passionfruit mojito. (☎080 146 3267; www.

995 Roasted Duck

🍽️

You may have to queue a while to get a seat at this glorified **shack** (Map p132, C4; mains from 70B; ⏰9am-9pm) in Sairee Village and wonder what all the fuss is about. The fuss is excellent and highly authentic Chinese roast duck, from 70B for a steaming bowl of roasted waterfowl with noodles to 700B for a whole bird, served in a jiffy by obliging staff. You'd be quackers to miss out.

barracudakohtao.com; Sairee Village; mains 240-380B; ⏰6-10.30pm; 📶)

Whitening

INTERNATIONAL $$

15 MAP P132, C6

This starched, white, beachy spot falls somewhere between being a restaurant and a chic seaside bar – foodies will appreciate the tasty twists on indigenous and international dishes. Dine amid dangling white Christmas lights while keeping your bare feet tucked into the sand. And the best part? It's comparatively easy on the wallet. (☎077 456199; Mae Hat; dishes 160-480B; ⏰1pm-1am; 📶)

Drinking

Lotus Bar

BAR

16 MAP P132, E7

Lotus is the leading late-night hang-out spot along the northern end of Sairee; it also affords front-row seats to some spectacular sunsets. Muscular fire-twirlers toss around flaming batons, and the drinks are so large there should be a lifeguard on duty. (☏087 069 6078; Sairee Beach)

Earth House BEER GARDEN

17 🍺 MAP P132, C6

This relaxing, secluded and rustic spot serves up a global selection of 40 beers, craft labels and ciders in a dreamy garden setting. With its own relaxing treehouse, there's also a restaurant for bites (open 9am to noon and 1pm to 6pm Monday to Saturday) – and there are bungalows alongside for going prone if you overdo it on the

Green Goblin (cider). (www.theearth housekohtao.com; ◷noon-midnight Mon-Sat)

Entertainment

Queen's Cabaret CABARET

18 ⭐ MAP P132, F7

Every night is different at this intimate bar where acts range from your standard sparkling Abba to steamy topless croons. If you're male, note you may get 'dragged' into the performance if you're sitting near the front. The show is free but it's expected that you will purchase a (pricey) drink – which is totally worth it. Show starts at 10.15pm. (☏087 677 6168; Sairee Village)

Shopping

Hammock Cafe Plaeyuan HOMEWARES

19 🔒 MAP P132, C7

This small French- and Thai-run cafe with tables out front on the road to Chalok Ban Kao doubles as a hammock shop, selling a fantastic selection of brightly coloured Mlabri hand-woven hammocks, some with up to 3km of fabric. Prices start at around 1700B for a sitting hammock, up to 5000B for the most elaborate. Attractive handmade jewellery is also for sale. (☏082 811 4312; ◷9am-6pm Sun-Fri)

Dive school on Ko Tao

AMNAT30/SHUTTERSTOCK ©

Dive Sites at a Glance

In general, divers don't have much of a choice as to which sites they explore. Each dive school chooses a smattering of sites for the day depending on weather and ocean conditions.

Chumphon Pinnacle (p128; 36m maximum depth) 11km northwest of Ko Tao, has a colourful assortment of sea anemones along the four interconnected pinnacles. The site plays host to schools of giant trevally, tuna and large grey reef sharks. Whale sharks are known to pop up once in a while.

Green Rock (Map p132, A1; 25m maximum depth) An underwater jungle gym featuring caverns, caves and small swim-throughs. Rays, grouper and triggerfish are known to hang around. It's a great place for a night dive.

Japanese Gardens (Map p132, B1; 12m maximum depth) Between Ko Tao and Ko Nang Yuan, is a low-stress dive site perfect for beginners. There's plenty of colourful coral, and turtles, stingray and pufferfish often pass by.

Mango Bay (Map p132, D1; 16m maximum depth) This might be your first dive site if you are putting on a tank for the first time. Lazy reef fish swim around as newbies practise their skills on the sandy bottom.

Lighthouse Bay (Gluay Teun Bay; Map p132, E2; 14m maximum depth), Also excellent for snorkelling, this bay is a shallow dive site on the northeastern tip of the island sporting some superb coral. Look out for yellowtail barracuda, parrotfish and bannerfish.

Sail Rock (p129; 40m maximum depth) Best accessed from Ko Pha-Ngan, features a massive rock chimney with a vertical swim-through, and large pelagics including barracuda and kingfish. This is one of the top spots in Southeast Asia to see whale sharks.

Southwest Pinnacle (p129; 28m maximum depth) Offers divers a small collection of pinnacles that are home to giant groupers and barracudas, and whale sharks are sometimes spotted.

White Rock (Map p132, B3; 29m maximum depth) Home to colourful corals, angelfish, clownfish and territorial triggerfish, and is a popular spot for night divers.

HTMS Sattakut (p129; 30m maximum depth) Was sunk southeast of Hin Pee Wee in 2011 at a depth of 30m and has become one of the most popular wreck diving sites.

Survival Guide

Before You Go

Book Your Stay

o If you're looking to splurge, there is definitely no shortage of top-end resorts sporting exclusive bungalows, pampering spas, private infinity pools and top-notch dining.

o Bo Phut, on the island's northern coast, has an attractive collection of boutique lodging – the perfect choice for midrange travellers.

o Backpack-lugging visitors may have to look a little harder, but budget digs pop up periodically along all of the island's beaches.

Useful Websites

Lonely Planet (www.lonelyplanet.com/hotels) Recommendations and bookings.

Best Budget

Dearly Koh Tao (☏ 077 332494; www.thedearly kohtaohostel.com; 14/55 Mu 3, Chalok Ban Kao; dm 600-700B, d 1700-3000B,

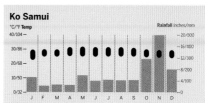

When to Go

o **High Season (late Dec–Jan, Jul & Aug)** Accommodation prices peak for Christmas and New Year; minimum stay at hotels during festive periods. Busy beaches with less space, more traffic on the roads.

o **Shoulder (Feb–Jun, Sep & Oct)** Quiet time to visit; some places are deserted. Accommodation prices are low.

o **Low Season (Nov–early Dec)** Rainy days and rough waves. Decent accommodation deals and bargains abound.

tr 2400B; ☏ ☀) Fab new hostel with all you need, plus a pool.

Coco Garden (☏ 077 377721, 086 073 1147; www.cocogardens.com; Thong Sala; bungalows 450-1100B; ❄ ☏) Excellent backpacker choice on Ko Pha-Ngan.

Earth House (www.theearthhouse-kohtao.com; 2/35 Mu 3; bungalows 350-600B; ☏) Away from the action, a hit with single travellers on Ko Tao.

New Hut (☏ 077 230437; Lamai North; huts 250-800B; ☏) Simple, unfussy and easy-going vibe on Ko Samui.

Smile Bungalows (☏ 085 429 4995; www.smilebungalows.com; Hat Khuat; bungalows 520-920B; ⊙ closed Nov) Remote, relaxed, all smiles on Bottle Beach.

Shangri-la (☏ 077 425189; Mae Nam; bungalows with fan/air-con from 500/1300B; ❄ ☏) Excellent value, on a fantastic stretch of Ko Samui sand.

Best Midrange

Jungle Club (☏ 081 894 2327; www.jungleclub samui.com; huts 800-1800B, houses 2700-4500B; ❄ @ 🛜 ☈) High up in the hills and away from it all on Ko Samui.

Mai Pen Rai (☏ 093 959 8073; www.thansadet.com; Than Sadet; bungalows 683-1365B; 🛜) End-of-the-world feel on the east coast of Ko Pha-Ngan.

Am Samui (☏ 077 423425; Taling Ngam; bungalows 1600-6000B; ❄ 🛜 ☈) Winning west coast Ko Samui setting.

Seetanu Bungalows (☏ 077 349113; www.seetanu.com; Ban Sri Thanu; bungalows 600-5000B; @ 🛜 ☈) Lovely location on the west coast of Ko Pha-Ngan and a fine bar.

Best Top End

Conrad Koh Samui (☏ 077 915888; www.conradkohsamui.com; villas 45,000-126,000B; ❄ 🛜 ☈) The last word in stylish, knock-out luxury living.

Four Seasons Koh Samui (☏ 077 243000; www.fourseasons.com/

kohsamui; Bang Po; villas from 36,500B; ❄ 🛜 ☈) Stunning views, top service and a superb beach.

Intercontinental Samui Baan Taling Ngam Resort (☏ 077 429100; www.samui.intercontinental.com; Taling Ngam; r from 12,000B; ❄ 🛜 ☈) Beautifully presented rooms paired with astonishing views.

Place (www.theplace kohtao.com; villas 8000-9000B; ❄ 🛜) Gorgeous, romantic choice on Ko Tao.

W Retreat Koh Samui (☏ 077 915999; www.wretreatkohsamui.com; Mae Nam; r from 20,000B; ❄ @ 🛜 ☈) Stylish comfort, effortless good looks and an awesome bar.

Jamahkiri Resort & Spa (☏ 077 456400; www.jamahkiri.com; Ao Thian Ok; bungalows incl breakfast 8400-30,000B; ❄ @ 🛜 ☈) Top choice on Ko Tao for full-on pampering and awesome views.

Sanctuary (☏ 081 271 3614; www.thesanctuary thailand.com; Hat Thian; 2000-7300B) Blissful remote haven on the east coast of Ko Pha-Ngan.

Arriving in Ko Samui

Air

Ko Samui's **airport** (www.samuiairportonline.com) is in the north-east of the island near Big Buddha Beach.

Bangkok Airways (www.bangkokair.com) operates flights roughly every 30 minutes between Samui and Bangkok's Suvarnabhumi International Airport (65 minutes). Bangkok Airways also flies direct from Samui to Phuket, Pattaya, Chiang Mai, Singapore, Kuala Lumpur, Hong Kong and other cities in Southeast Asia. Bangkok Airways also flies to Chéngdū and Guǎngzhōu in China.

There is a **Bangkok Airways Office** (☏ 077 420512, 077 420519; www.bangkokair.com) in Hat Chaweng and another at the airport. The first (at 6am) and last (10pm) flights of the day are always the cheapest.

Sea

To reach Samui, the main piers on the mainland are Ao Ban Don, Tha Thong, Don Sak and Chumphon – Tha Thong (in central Surat) and Don Sak being the most common. On Samui, the three most used ports are Na Thon, Mae Nam and Big Buddha Beach. Expect complimentary taxi transfers with high-speed ferry services.

To the Mainland

There are regular boat departures between Samui and Don Sak on the mainland.

High-speed **Lomprayah** (☏ 077 4277 656; www.lomprayah.com) ferries depart from Na Thon (400B; 8am, 9.45am, 12.45pm & 3.30pm) and take just 45 minutes; some departures can connect with the train station in Phun Phin (600B) for Surat Thani.

There's also the slower but regular **Raja** (☏ 022 768211-2, 092 274 3423-5; www.raja ferryport.com; adult 130B) car ferry (130B; 90

minutes) to Don Sak, which departs from Thong Yang. The slow night boat to Samui (300B) leaves from central Surat Thani each night at 11pm, reaching Na Thon around 5am. It returns from Na Thon at 9pm, arriving at around 3am. Watch your bags on this boat.

Lomprayah ferries also depart from Pralarn Pier in Mae Nam for Chumphon (1100B; 8am and 12.30pm; 3¾ hours).

To Ko Pha-Ngan & Ko Tao

There are almost a dozen daily departures between Ko Samui and Thong Sala on the west coast of Ko Pha-Ngan, and many of these continue on to Ko Tao. These leave from Na Thon, Pralarn Pier in Mae Nam or Big Buddha Beach pier, take from 20 minutes to one hour and cost 200B to 300B to Ko Pha-Ngan, depending on the boat.

To go directly to Hat Rin, the *Haad Rin*

Queen goes back and forth between Hat Rin and Big Buddha Beach four times a day (the first boat leaves Hat Rin at 9.30am and departs Big Buddha Beach at 10.30am), with double the number of sailings the day after the Full Moon Party and an extra trip laid on at 7.30am the same day. The voyage takes 50 minutes, costs 200B and the last boat leaves Big Buddha Beach at 6.30pm.

Also for Hat Rin and the more remote east coast beaches of Ko Pha-Ngan, the small and rickety *Thong Nai Pan Express* runs once a day at noon from Mae Hat on Ko Samui to Hat Rin and then up the east coast, stopping at all the beaches as far as Thong Nai Pan Noi. Prices range from 200B to 400B, depending on the destination. The boat won't run in bad weather.

Electricity

Essential Information

Type A
220V/50Hz

Type C
220V/50Hz

Business Hours

Banks
9.30am to 3.30pm
Monday to Friday

Bars & Clubs
Many open till 2am,
though the military
periodically forces
them to shut at 1am

Restaurants
Typically 9am or 10am
to 11pm or midnight,
but can vary

Government Offices
8.30am to 4.30pm
Monday to Friday.
Some also close for
lunch

Shops
Typically 9am to
10pm, but can vary

Money

ATMs are widely available. Credit cards are accepted in most hotels and restaurants.

ATMs

o Most ATMs will charge a 220B foreign transaction fee on top

of your bank's currency conversion fees, no matter how much you withdraw.

Cash

o The basic unit of Thai currency is the baht (B).

o Notes come in denominations of 20B, 50B, 100B, 500B and 1000B, while coins come in 1B, 2B, 5B and 10B and occasionally 25 satang or 50 satang.

Changing Money

o Changing money isn't a problem on the

Money-Saving Tips

o Avoid buying paracetamol, sunscreen and insect repellent from pharmacies – try convenience stores such as 7-Eleven.

o Avoid taking out small sums of money from ATMs to reduce usage fees.

o Visit during the low season when prices are low, as sre visitor numbers.

east and north coasts, and in Na Thon. In Chaweng, every other shop is a money exchange, with the 'best rate'.

Credit Cards

o Credit and debit cards can be used in most shops and at most hotels and restaurants.

o Notify your bank and credit-card provider before your trip so they are aware you will be in Thailand.

Exchange Rates

Australia	AS$	23B
Canada	C$1	27B
EU	€1	38B
Japan	¥100	28B
NZ	NZ$1	24B
UK	£1	43B
US	US$1	31B

For current exchange rates, see www.xe.com

Tipping

o Tipping is not generally expected, though it is certainly appreciated. Check, though, if a 10% service charge has been added to your bill.

Public Holidays

Lunar holidays change each year; check out the website of the **Tourism Authority of Thailand** (TAT; www.tatnews.org).

New Year's Day 1 January

Magha Puja Lunar holiday in February or March

Chakri Day 6 April

Songkran 13 to 15 April

Coronation Day 5 May

Visakha Puja Lunar holiday in May

Asalha Puja Lunar holiday in July

Khao Phansa Lunar holiday in July

King's Birthday 28 July

Queen's Birthday 12 August

Chulalongkorn Day 23 October

Constitution Day 10 December

Safe Travel

o The road-accident fatality rate on Ko Samui is high, largely because of the significant number of (inexperienced) tourist drivers who

rent motorcycles and scooters. Drive slowly at all times and wear a helmet.

o Look out for glass on less-visited beaches – a lot of broken glass (from discarded beer and soda bottles) lies on the sands.

o See the box on page (p121) on box jellyfish, a potentially lethal danger lurking in the sea waters of the Lower Gulf.

o If caught in a rip tide (a strong surface current heading seaward), it is advised not to fight it and rapidly tire, but instead to swim parallel to the shore to exit the current or float along with it until it dissipates in deeper water and you are deposited.

Toilets

In many smaller bars and restaurants, the toilet system is not equipped to deal with toilet paper, in which case a bin or basket is provided for the purpose. Many toilets also come with a small spray hose, as in Malaysia, which serves as a kind of flexible bidet.

Tourist Information

There is no official tourist office on Ko Samui. Tourist information is largely provided by hotels and travel agents.

The **Siam Map Company** (www.siammap.com) puts out quarterly booklets including a Spa Guide, Dining Guide and an annual directory, which lists thousands of companies and hotels on Ko Samui. Its *Samui Guide Map* is found throughout the island.

Travellers with Disabilities

The infrastructure in Samui is rather basic, such that few areas and businesses are accessible beyond the more expensive hotels. Movement around Samui can be difficult in a wheelchair: footpaths are limited, crowded and rarely have kerb cutaways.

For more information on accessible travel, visit http:// lptravel.to/Accessible Travel.

Visas

Citizens of 62 countries, including Australia, Canada, New Zealand, South Africa, the UK and the USA can stay in Thailand for 30 days without a visa. If you plan to stay more than 30 days, you will need to apply for a 60-day visa.

Visa Extensions

The new **Immigration Office** (077 423440; Soi 1 Mu 1, Mae Nam; 8.30am-4.30pm Mon-Fri) is located south of the 4169 in Mae Nam.

Dos & Don'ts

Thai people are generally very understanding and hospitable, but there are some important taboos and social conventions you need to understand.

o **Monarchy** Never disrespect the royal family with disparaging remarks and always treat objects carrying the royal symbols and portraits with respect. Stand when the national and king's anthems are played.

o **Temples** Wear clothing that reaches to your knees and elbows. Remove your shoes when entering a temple hall. Sit with your feet tucked behind you to avoid pointing the bottom of your feet at images of Buddha. Women should never touch a monk or a monk's belongings; step out of the way of monks on footpaths and don't sit next to them on public transport.

o **Modesty** At the beach, avoid public nudity and topless sunbathing. Wear a cover-up to and from the beach.

o **Saving Face** Never get into an argument with a Thai. It is better to smile through any conflict.

Language

In Thai the meaning of a single syllable may be altered by means of different tones. Standard Thai has five tones: low (eg *bàht*), mid (eg *dee*), falling (eg *mâi*), high (eg *máh*) and rising (eg *săhm*). The range of all five tones is relative to each speaker's vocal range, so there is no fixed 'pitch' intrinsic to the language.

Read our pronunciation guides as if they were English and you'll be understood. The hyphens indicate syllable breaks; some syllables are further divided with a dot to help you pronounce compound vowels (eg *mêu·a·rai*). Note that **ʰ** is a hard 'p' sound, almost like a 'b' (eg in 'hip-bag'); **đ** is a hard 't' sound, like a sharp 'd' (eg in 'mid-tone'); **ng** is pronounced as in 'singing', but in Thai it can also occur at the start of a word; and **r** is pronounced as in 'run' but flapped, and in everyday speech it's often pronounced like 'l'.

To enhance your trip with a phrasebook, visit **lonelyplanet.com**. Lonely Planet iPhone phrasebooks are available through the Apple App store.

Basics

Hello.	สวัสดี	*sà-wàt-dee*
Goodbye.	ลาก่อน	*lah gòrn*
Yes./No.	ใช่/ไม่	*châi/mâi*
Please.	ขอ	*kŏr*
Thank you.	ขอบคุณ	*kòrp kun*

You're welcome.	ยินดี	*yin dee*
Excuse me.	ขออภัย	*kŏr à-pai*
Sorry.	ขอโทษ	*kŏr tôht*

How are you?
สบายดีไหม   *sà-bai dee măi*

Fine. And you?
สบายดีครับ/ค่ะ   *sà-bai dee kráp/*
แล้วคุณล่ะ   *kâ láa·ou kun lâ* (m/f)

Do you speak English?
คุณพูดภาษา   *kun pôot pah-săh*
อังกฤษได้ไหม   *ang-grìt dâi măi*

I don't understand.
ผม/ดิฉันไม่   *pŏm/dì-chăn mâi*
เข้าใจ   *kôw jai* (m/f)

Eating & Drinking

I'd like (the menu), please.
ขอ (รายการ   *kŏr (rai gahn*
อาหาร) หน่อย   *ah-hăhn) nòy*

I don't eat ...
ผม/ดิฉัน   *pŏm/dì-chăn*
ไม่กิน ...   *mâi gin ...* (m/f)

eggs	ไข่	*kài*
fish	ปลา	*ʰlah*
red meat	เนื้อแดง	*néu·a daang*
nuts	ถั่ว	*tòo·a*

That was delicious!
อร่อยมาก   *à-ròy mâhk*

Cheers!
ไชโย — *chai-yoh*

Please bring the bill.
ขอบิลหน่อย — *kŏr bin nòy*

cafe	ร้านกาแฟ	*ráhn gah-faa*
market	ตลาด	*đà-làht*
restaurant	ร้านอาหาร	*ráhn ah-hăhn*
vegetarian	เจ	*jair*

Meat & Fish

beef	เนื้อ	*néu·a*
chicken	ไก่	*gài*
crab	ปู	*ʉoo*
duck	เป็ด	*ʉèt*
fish	ปลา	*ʉlah*
meat	เนื้อ	*néu·a*
pork	หมู	*mŏo*
seafood	อาหารทะเล	*ah-hăhn tá-lair*
squid	ปลาหมึก	*ʉlah mèuk*

Fruit & Vegetables

banana	กล้วย	*glôo·ay*
beans	ถั่ว	*tòo·a*
coconut	มะพร้าว	*má-prów*
eggplant	มะเขือ	*má-kěu·a*
fruit	ผลไม้	*pŏn-lá-mái*
guava	ฝรั่ง	*fa-ràng*
lime	มะนาว	*má-now*
mango	มะม่วง	*má-môo·ang*
mangosteen	มังคุด	*mang-kút*
mushrooms	เห็ด	*hèt*
nuts	ถั่ว	*tòo·a*

papaya	มะละกอ	*má-lá-gor*
potatoes	มันฝรั่ง	*man fa-ràng*
rambutan	เงาะ	*ngó*
tamarind	มะขาม	*má-kăhm*
tomatoes	มะเขือเทศ	*má-kěu·a têt*
vegetables	ผัก	*pàk*
watermelon	แตงโม	*đaang moh*

Drinks

beer	เบียร์	*bee·a*
coffee	กาแฟ	*gah-faa*
milk	นมจืด	*nom jèut*
orange juice	น้ำส้ม	*nám sôm*
soy milk	น้ำเต้าหู้	*nám đôw hôo*
sugar-cane juice	น้ำอ้อย	*nám ôy*
tea	ชา	*chah*
water	น้ำดื่ม	*nám dèum*

Other

chilli	พริก	*prík*
egg	ไข่	*kài*
fish sauce	น้ำปลา	*nám ʉlah*
noodles	เส้น	*sên*
pepper	พริกไทย	*prík tai*
rice	ข้าว	*kôw*
salad	ผักสด	*pàk sòt*
salt	เกลือ	*gleu·a*
soup	น้ำซุป	*nám súp*
soy sauce	น้ำซีอิ๊ว	*nám see-éw*
sugar	น้ำตาล	*nám đahn*
tofu	เต้าหู้	*đôw hôo*

Shopping

I'd like to buy ...
อยากจะซื้อ ...　　　*yàhk jà séu ...*

How much is it?
เท่าไร　　　*tôw-rai*

That's too expensive.
แพงไป　　　*paang bai*

Can you lower the price?
ลดราคาได้ไหม　　*lót rah-kah dâi măi*

There's a mistake in the bill.
บิลใบนี้ผิด　　　*bin bai née pìt ná*
นะครับ/ค่ะ　　　*kráp/kâ (m/f)*

Emergencies

Help!　　ช่วยด้วย　　*chôo·ay*
　　　　　　　　　　　　dôo·ay

Go away!　ไปให้พ้น　*bai hâi pón*

Call a doctor!
เรียกหมอหน่อย　　*rêe·ak mŏr nòy*

Call the police!
เรียกตำรวจ　　　*rêe·ak đam·ròo·at*
หน่อย　　　　　　*nòy*

I'm ill.
ผม/ดิฉัน　　　*pŏm/dì-chăn*
ป่วย　　　　　*bòo·ay (m/f)*

I'm lost.
ผม/ดิฉัน　　　*pŏm/dì-chăn*
หลงทาง　　　*lŏng tahng (m/f)*

Where are the toilets?
ห้องน้ำ　　　*hôrng nám*
อยู่ที่ไหน　　*yòo têe năi*

Time, Days & Numbers

What time is it?
กี่โมงแล้ว　　　*gèe mohng láa·ou*

morning	เช้า	*chów*
afternoon	บ่าย	*bài*
evening	เย็น	*yen*
yesterday	เมื่อวาน	*mêu·a wahn*
today	วันนี้	*wan née*
tomorrow	พรุ่งนี้	*prûng née*
Monday	วันจันทร์	*wan jan*
Tuesday	วันอังคาร	*wan ang-kahn*
Wednesday	วันพุธ	*wan pút*
Thursday	วันพฤหัสฯ	*wan pá-réu-hàt*
Friday	วันศุกร	*wan sùk*
Saturday	วันเสาร์	*wan sŏw*
Sunday	วันอาทิตย์	*wan ah-tít*
1	หนึ่ง	*nèung*
2	สอง	*sŏrng*
3	สาม	*săhm*
4	สี่	*sèe*
5	ห้า	*hâh*
6	หก	*hòk*
7	เจ็ด	*jèt*
8	แปด	*bàat*
9	เก้า	*gôw*
10	สิบ	*sìp*

20	ยี่สิบ	*yêe-sìp*
21	ยี่สิบเอ็ด	*yêe-sìp-èt*
30	สามสิบ	*săhm-sìp*
40	สี่สิบ	*sèe-sìp*
50	ห้าสิบ	*hâh-sìp*
60	หกสิบ	*hòk-sìp*
70	เจ็ดสิบ	*jèt-sìp*
80	แปดสิบ	*ɓàat-sìp*
90	เก้าสิบ	*gôw-sìp*
100	หนึ่งร้อย	*nèung róy*
1000	หนึ่งพัน	*nèung pan*
1,000,000	หนึ่งล้าน	*nèung láhn*

Transport & Directions

Where is ...?
... อยู่ที่ไหน   *... yòo têe năi*

What's the address?
ที่อยู่คืออะไร   *têe yòo keu à-rai*

Can you show me (on the map)?
ให้ดู (ในแผนที่)   *hâi doo (nai păn têe)*
ได้ไหม   *dâi măi*

Turn left/right.
เลี้ยวซ้าย/ขวา   *lée·o sái/kwăh*

bicycle rickshaw	สามล้อ	*săhm lór*
boat	เรือ	*reu·a*
bus	รถเมล์	*rót mair*
car	รถเก๋ง	*rót gĕng*
motorcycle	มอร์เตอร์ไซค์	*mor-đeu-sai*
taxi	รถแท็กซี่	*rót táak·sêe*
plane	เครื่องบิน	*krêu·ang bin*
train	รถไฟ	*rót fai*
túk-túk	ตุ๊ก ๆ	*đúk đúk*

When's the first bus?
รถเมล์คันแรก   *rót mair kan râak*
มาเมื่อไร   *mah mêu·a rai*

A (one-way/return) ticket, please.
ขอตั๋ว (เที่ยว   *kŏr đŏo·a (têe·o*
เดียว/ไปกลับ).   *dee·o/ɓai glàp)*

What time does it get to ...?
ถึง ... กี่โมง   *tĕung ... gèe mohng*

Does it stop at ...?
รถจอดที่ ... ไหม   *rót jòrt têe ... măi*

I'd like to get off at ...
ขอลงที่ ...   *kŏr long têe ...*

Index

See also separate subindexes for:

✖ **Eating p155**

🍷 **Drinking p156**

🎭 **Entertainment p156**

🛍 **Shopping p156**

🛌 **Sleeping p157**

Experiences 000
Map Pages 000

Behind the Scenes

Send Us Your Feedback

We love to hear from travellers – your comments help make our books better. We read every word, and we guarantee that your feedback goes straight to the authors. Visit **lonelyplanet.com/contact** to submit your updates and suggestions.

Note: We may edit, reproduce and incorporate your comments in Lonely Planet products such as guidebooks, websites and digital products, so let us know if you don't want your comments reproduced or your name acknowledged. For a copy of our privacy policy visit lonelyplanet.com/privacy.

Damian's Thanks

Huge thanks to the late Neil Bambridge, much gratitude for everything, may you rest in peace. Also thanks to Neil's wife Ratchi, to Maurice Senseit, the jolly staff at Nira's in Thong Sala, Piotr, Gemma, James Horton, George W, Celeste Brash and everyone else who helped along the way, in whatever fashion.

Acknowledgements

Cover photo: Fishing boat, Coral Cove Beach, Ko Samui, Josef Beck/Alamy ©

Photographs pp28–9 (from left): Logan Brown/Getty Images; Sasiphoto/Shutterstock; Parasola Parasola/Getty Images; Dkart/Getty Images ©

This Book

This 2nd edition of Lonely Planet's *Pocket Ko Samui* guidebook was researched and written by Damian Harper. The previous edition (*Encounter Ko Samui*) was written by China Williams. This guidebook was produced by the following:

Destination Editors
Tanya Parker,
Clifton Wilkinson

Series Designer
Campbell McKenzie

Cartographic Series Designer Wayne Murphy

Senior Product Editor
Kate Chapman

Product Editors
Amanda Williamson,
Alison Ridgway

Senior Cartographer
Diana von Holdt

Book Designer
Meri Blazevski

Cartographer
Julie Dodkins

Assisting Editors Judith Bamber, Michelle Bennett, Victoria Harrison

Cover Researchers
Brendan Dempsey-Spencer, Naomi Parker

Thanks to Imogen Bannister, Laura Crawford, Shona Gray, Blaze Hadzik, James Hardy, Liz Heynes, Simon Hoskins, Chris Lee Ack, Jean-Pierre Masclef, Liam McGrellis, Dan Moore, Virginia Moreno, Darren O'Connell, Martine Power, Kirsten Rawlings, Wibowo Rusli, Dianne Schallmeiner, Ellie Simpson, John Taufa, Angela Tinson, Juan Winata

Our Writer

Damian Harper

With two degrees (one in modern and classical Chinese from SOAS University of London), Damian has been writing for Lonely Planet for more than two decades, contributing to titles on places as diverse as China, Vietnam, Thailand, Ireland, London, Mallorca, Malaysia, Singapore, Brunei, Hong Kong and the UK. A seasoned guidebook writer, Damian has penned articles for numerous newspapers and magazines, including the *Guardian* and the *Daily Telegraph*, and currently makes Surrey, England, his home.

Follow Damian on Instagram @damian.harper.

Published by Lonely Planet Global Limited
CRN 554153
2nd edition – October 2018
ISBN 978 1 78701 263 9
© Lonely Planet 2018   Photographs © as indicated 2018
10 9 8 7 6 5 4 3 2 1
Printed in Singapore